P9-CWD-895

THE POLITICS OF PETULANCE

THE POLITICS OF PETULANCE

America in an Age of Immaturity

ALAN WOLFE

The University of Chicago Press
Chicago and London

The University of Chicago Press, Chicago 60637
The University of Chicago Press, Ltd., London

Published 2018
Printed in the United States of America

27 26 25 24 23 22 21 20 19 18   1 2 3 4 5

ISBN-13: 978-0-226-55516-4 (cloth)
ISBN-13: 978-0-226-55533-1 (e-book)
DOI: https://doi.org/10.7208/chicago/9780226555331.001.0001

Library of Congress Cataloging-in-Publication Data

Names: Wolfe, Alan, 1942– author.
Title: The politics of petulance : America in an age of immaturity / Alan Wolfe.
Description: Chicago : The University of Chicago Press, 2018. | Includes bibliographical references and index.
Identifiers: LCCN 2018010072 | ISBN 9780226555164 (cloth : alk. paper) | ISBN 9780226555331 (e-book)
Subjects: LCSH: Liberalism—United States. | United States—Politics and government—21st century. | Politics, Practical—United States. | Democracy—United States. | Populism—United States.
Classification: LCC JC574.2.U6 W67 2018 | DDC 320.51/30973—dc23
LC record available at https://lccn.loc.gov /2018010072

♾ This paper meets the requirements of ANSI/NISO Z39.48-1992 (Permanence of Paper).

For Maya,
who has renewed my hopes for the future

CONTENTS

ACKNOWLEDGMENTS

This book is a product of numerous discussions with my literary agent, Andrew Stuart. Although it has grown into a product quite different from what he and I imagined in the beginning, it never would have been undertaken without his encouragement. Even more, Andrew put me in touch with Timothy Mennel at the University of Chicago Press, and he and I knew right off the bat what kind of book was needed. He also worked in superhuman fashion to get this book published in a timely manner. I also had confidence in the press because of my previous collaborations with Doug Mitchell and Chuck Myers. I know I have the perfect publisher for my venture. Let me also express my gratitude to the two readers relied upon by the press; to Marian Rogers, who did a masterful job with the editing; to Sergey Lobachev for the indexing; and to Susan Karani for expediting the production of this book.

Nat Glazer, the only one of the group about which I write who is still alive, read and offered extensive comments on the manuscript. Sanford Levinson, Howard Gardner, and Michael St. Clair are wonderful conversational companions. Enid Beal is the most perfect "partner"—girlfriend sounds a little silly, and we don't have any other term—a man could wish for. Anything I say here will be trite compared to what I feel for her in my heart.

My first grandchild, Maya Elise Berengaut, was born soon before I began writing. This book is dedicated to her.

1
MATURE LIBERALISM

Had Donald J. Trump, a man with obvious authoritarian proclivities, achieved the presidency through authoritarian means, we would have had to acknowledge a serious flaw in our electoral system. But he achieved it through democratic means, which suggests that there is a serious flaw within us.

When any future ranking of America's worst presidents is published, Donald Trump's name will appear there. The only open question is whether he will top the list, given that James Buchanan and Andrew Johnson are already on it. Listing every boast Trump made, every lie he told, every slander he directed at his opposition, every humiliating remark he made or action he took against women, every fact of history of which he was unaware, every foreign leader he demeaned, every racist he defended, and every paranoid conspiracy theory he endorsed might well produce a book in itself. Instead let me proceed on the assumption that the mere mention of his name conjures up for most of my readers sufficiently horrific associations that the burning question immediately becomes not how he got himself elected, but why, of all the potential leaders available to them, Americans chose this particular one as their president.

Pundits explain Trump's victory away by pointing to the money provided by his wealthy backers, the allegedly poor campaign run by his opponent, the help he received knowingly or unknowingly from Russia, the false equivalency relied upon by the media, the unprecedented intervention of the FBI, even the misuse of social media. If only matters were so simple. The unhappy fact is that Trump was elected, and elected fairly, by the American people. He entered a crowded field for the Republican nomination and defeated all his many rivals, quite decisively, and without any election rigging. In a society that relies, rightly or wrongly, on the Electoral College to decide the winner, he won the necessary electoral votes as well, and by a substantial margin. Trump is right to linger on the success of his 2016 campaign. It may not have been possible to predict all the trouble in which Trump found himself after his election, but a great deal was already known about his shady business dealings, his refusal to release his tax returns, his overt bigotry, his bragging about his sexual conquests, his ignorance of the wider world, and his personal cruelty to anyone who stood in his way. He won because at least some found him attractive anyway.

Perhaps Americans, realizing that they made a serious mistake in 2016, will come to regret their decision. Perhaps Trump will serve only one term, or even, depending upon the results of the investigations surrounding him, less. The hard core of his base may at some point tire of him. Or he may tire of them. But the fact of his victory is what counts. It cannot be taken away or excused away. It is a brutal reality, the single most important political event in the United States since JFK's victory in 1960, if not FDR's election to a first term in 1932. There is no way to pretend it did not happen, and no way, at least no easy way, to overcome the damage it has already done to the reputation of our country. If Trump's accession to the presidency does not cause intense introspection, nothing can. It is, furthermore, not an explanation of one rogue election we need. It is a discussion of what kind of nation we have become.

All too often, at crucial points in their history, Americans find themselves responding to demagogues: Henry Ford, Huey Long, Father Charles Coughlin, Theodore Bilbo, Joseph McCarthy, George Wallace, Spiro Agnew, Patrick Buchanan, Sarah Palin, Roy Moore, and now the president himself are all examples. A demagogue is a politician who appeals to people's unreflective emotions and relies on a simplistic worldview to win and hold office by any means necessary. Not all of our politicians are demagogues: Barack Obama, whatever else one thinks of him, with his heightened sense of irony and innate political centrism, was the very opposite of a demagogue (except to critics on the right such as Charles Krauthammer).[1] Hillary Clinton was too predictable to be a demagogue, and Mike Pence, despite extremely right-wing views, is too lacking in charisma to be one. Whether we have elected too many for our good is for each person to decide; in my opinion, we risk danger to ourselves and to our institutions every time we choose one. The 2016 election was not unprecedented: it was the culmination of a series of elections that have deviated from meaningful conceptions of the democratic ideal, except that this one resulted in the choice of a president the likes of which we will likely never see again in American public life. All demagogues resemble each other, but the one chosen as president in 2016 still found a way to be sui generis.

What makes Donald Trump unique, even among all other demagogues in our history, or so I will argue in the book that follows, is that he has revealed for all to see why demagogues happen: the demagogic style flourishes as a substitute for mature leadership. Demagoguery is a near-perfect expression of what I am calling the politics of petulance. Like a snake-oil salesman, the demagogue discovers the susceptibility of the people to nostrums of relief designed to distract them from the real causes of their worries. In the demagogue's world, emotions take precedence over facts, remedies are hastily assembled, policies are promoted irrespective of their consequences, enemies are identified, scores are settled, crimes become common, distractions are offered, and when none of these remedies seem to work, as they invariably do not, the leader and the people, joined together in mutual frustration, lash out like six-year-olds at a world beyond their ability to comprehend. Most demagogues never reach the pinnacle of power; their strength and appeal lie in being an outlet for protest. Now, by contrast, we have a demagogue holding the most powerful position in the country and maybe even the world. Is it any wonder that no one seems to know exactly what he, or we, will do?

Fortunately for us, demagoguery is a well-studied subject. Because we have had demagogues before in our history, we also have a body of literature seeking to understand them. Joe McCarthy, the Communist-hunting senator from Wisconsin, followed so quickly after his demise by the radical right that nominated Barry Goldwater as the Republican candidate for president in 1964, provided the most sustained attempt we have to understand the "moments of madness" that from time to time overtake our politics.[2] The thinkers who provided us with insights into the meaning and significance of the McCarthy years were trained in different disciplines: literary criticism, history, the social sciences, and theology. They were nonetheless united by their insistence that a well-functioning political system requires an ability to say no to unfiltered desires in the name of some future goal. That is exactly what the Joe McCarthy and the Goldwater right were missing. Their impulsivity, their search for scapegoats, their simplicity, and above all else their irremediable petulance—all revealed an approach to politics lacking in personal and political growth.

We are living now with so much wrong in our politics because we failed to heed the warnings of those who tried to make sense of the last time the United States became obsessed with demons that did not exist and turned to a charlatan to make them go away. One can only hope that it is not too late to learn what to do when demagoguery threatens.

The words *demagoguery* and *democracy* both originated in ancient Greece, and the questions I am asking about their relationship are among the oldest in political theory. In book 5 of his *Politics*, Aristotle wrote that "in democracies changes are chiefly due to the wanton license of demagogues. This takes two forms. Sometimes they attack the rich individually, by bringing false accusations, and thus force them to combine (for a common danger unites even the bitterest enemies); sometimes they attack them as a class, by egging on the people against them."[3] This was a lesson fully absorbed by the American founders, most of whom knew the writings of the Greeks and Romans intimately. How, you might wonder, would Publius, the name used to characterize the three authors of the brilliant Federalist Papers, bring the wisdom of all eighty-five chapters to an end? Alexander Hamilton, who is much admired on Broadway these days, wrote that last chapter, and in its very last paragraph, he cited philosopher David Hume before adding this: "These judicious reflections contain a lesson of moderation to all the sincere lovers of the Union, and ought to put them upon their guard against hazarding anarchy, civil war, a perpetual alienation of the states from each other, and perhaps the military despotism of a victorious demagogue, in the pursuit of what they are not likely to obtain, but from time and experience."[4] Contributing his thoughts a few decades later, Alexis de Tocqueville did not write extensively about demagogues, using the term only twice in *Democracy in America*. But he did worry a great deal about despots: "Despotism, then, which is at all times dangerous, is more particularly to be feared in democratic ages."[5] At times, Tocqueville believed, the passion for equality in America could turn into a raging fury, and at those times, a restraining force would become necessary. Despotism is dangerous because American democracy, without an aristocracy such as there was in France, lacks any such restraints.

Although worries about demagogues are centuries old, an admission of their existence can be taken as too severe a criticism of the society that produces them. That may be why, in the years after the end of World War II, with the Great Depression finally over and some kind of peace seemingly in hand, the country experienced what the sociologist C. Wright Mills called the "new American celebration."[6] To the extent that demagogues were discussed during these relatively placid years, they were treated as outside the pale: lonely, even if rather colorful, figures lacking a national following, whose influence was therefore containable. The single best treatment of the demagogic style back then was Robert Penn Warren's novel *All the King's Men*, based on the figure of Huey Long, published in 1946 and transformed into a masterful film three years later; the figure of Willy Stark realistically conveys both the dreams he held out to his followers as well as the nightmares that followed from his corruption and short-sightedness.

Warren wrote fiction; in matters of fact, it was widely believed in the early postwar years that we were too good a society to nurture too many bad characters. Demagogues were seen as products of unusual periods such as the Great Depression, which did indeed produce, in addition to Huey Long and Fr. Coughlin, the anti-Semite Gerald L. K. Smith, the agrarian radical William Lemke, Francis Everett Townsend and his plan for pensions for all older Americans, as well as the delightfully named California version of the same thing called "the ham and eggs movement." All of these demagogues, save Huey Long, who had been assassinated, created the Union Party—let's call it "Demagogues United"—and nominated Lemke as their candidate for president in 1936. The party's overwhelming defeat suggested that perhaps demagoguery itself was finally finished. Given sufficient calm abroad and at home, which optimists felt would follow in the postwar period, we might never have to face demagogues again.

This optimism suffused not just popular culture but the writing of history. The future Librarian of Congress Daniel Boorstin wrote in *The Genius of American Politics* that Americans were pragmatists who instinctively feel uncomfortable with implacable pronouncements, dogmatic declarations, and dug-in sectarianism.[7] Unlike European countries, this one never served as a home to serious political philosophers, he argued, mostly because it did not need them: the American way of life gave people all they needed to address their problems at home and abroad. From such a perspective, the Civil War was not a clash between two different moral conceptions of the good life, one slave and one free, but an argument over points of constitutional interpretation. Politics and religion, furthermore, were not at war with each other, because both sought "a kind of lowest common denominator."[8] No demagogues appear in Boorstin's book. Though the lectures on which it was based were given while Senator Joseph McCarthy was running amok, Boorstin never paused to reflect on the anti-Communist crusade and what it might mean. "Genius," in my view, was as poorly chosen a term as one could find to characterize American politics in the 1950s. So lacking in any kind of critical analysis was Boorstin's book that he was quickly labeled a follower of "consensus history,"[9] and the term rightly stuck: there are no hints of Madisonian or Hamiltonian pessimism, any dash of Lincoln's tragic realism, or any mention of the South's thirst for vengeance in this fairy-tale treatment of American political history. In his view, as in many others, demagoguery just couldn't happen here.

Yet Joe McCarthy offered living proof of our lack of political genius. As demagogues go, the senator from Wisconsin had quite a remarkable run. He had had no experience in political life before his first (successful) run for the Senate in 1946. Once elected, as his biographer David M. Oshinsky wrote, "every time he took to the floor to speak, trouble seemed to follow. Harried colleagues accused him of lying, manipulating figures, playing fast and loose with the Senate's most cherished traditions."[10] He was a notorious liar willing to say anything that he thought would advance his cause. His language "was shrill and exaggerated. . . . Words like 'fantastic,' 'unheard of,' 'sensational,' 'unbelievable,' and 'incredible' jumped from the pages." He saw conspiracies everywhere. Very few liked him; many more feared him. Although his staff prepared his speeches, he inevitably departed from the text to settle scores and launch accusations. He hated the press, which usually returned the favor, although he did show a genius for manipulating it. For all his success, politics was not really his bailiwick: "Reckless, uncompromising, bored with detail," as Oshinsky puts it, "he was ill-suited for law-making."[11] If all this sounds familiar, perhaps that is because the demagogue, like the harlequin in a *commedia dell'arte* performance, is now a stock character in the larger comedy called contemporary American politics.

The McCarthy period and the radical right posed a fundamental challenge to those whose business it was to understand America. Scholars like Boorstin chose one path. Richard Hofstadter, although wrongly identified as a consensus historian, chose a radically different one: he searched for an explanation of the historical roots of the frenzy that characterized American politics during the 1950s and 1960s. Hofstadter, who sat in the very center of the group that sought to treat postwar American politics out of a fear of irresponsible demagoguery, remains essential reading to us today, as Boorstin does not, because he made a serious attempt to return to the questions asked by Aristotle, America's founders, and Tocqueville about the relationship between democracy and demagoguery. If there is any key to understanding just how Donald Trump became our president, it can be found among the ideas of Hofstadter and his friends, colleagues, and contemporaries.

For Hofstadter and others, the Great Depression, World War II, totalitarianism, the Moscow purge trials, the Stalinist Gulag, and the Holocaust, however dreadful for the people who experienced them, were high times for political theory. Cruelty, racism, violence, authority, power, retribution, nationalism, mass society, propaganda, terror, imperialism, human nature, and international justice—these are only some of the subjects to which thoughtful scholars and intellectuals turned in the years after World War II. The writers who emerged to reflect on these matters had unusual depth and wisdom. They were the first generation of intellectuals, at any time in the history of the world, to ponder the problem of statehood in the wake of the atomic bomb. The war these men and women fought was a cold one, in which victory would be determined by ideas, and they were convinced, rightly as it happened, that their side had the better ones. These individuals were, I believe, the wisest group of political thinkers to appear in this country since the intellectuals who created it and wrote its founding documents.

Many of the political thinkers who made a name for themselves in the years following World War II had been born in Europe, including Hannah Arendt, Joseph Schumpeter, Fritz Stern, Erich Fromm, Karl Polanyi, Judith Shklar, Hans Kohn, Carl J. Friedrich, Hans Gerth, Saul Friedländer, Franz Neumann, and Czesław Miłosz. (It is possible to name many, many others.) They had direct knowledge of the madness into which countries can descend. The story of how émigré scholars enriched American academic and intellectual life has been told many times: their lives and work testify that a country that opens itself to the world receives wondrous benefits in return. Yet often forgotten is how little impact they actually had on the political life of their adopted country. Indeed, many of them, as the sociologist Louis A. Coser (himself an émigré) pointed out, spent their time here translating German thinkers such as Max Weber and Karl Mannheim for an American audience.[12]

With the exceptions of Arendt and Shklar, none of the émigré European thinkers were especially helpful in understanding American liberalism—seemingly the key to any appreciation of the American experience—and only Schumpeter was important in helping his adopted country understand democracy. Indeed, the most influential of the émigrés were of a conservative or libertarian disposition, including, in addition to Schumpeter, Leo Strauss, Eric Voegelin, Friedrich von Hayek, Ludwig von Mises, John Lukacs, and a host of other contributors to the early years of *National Review*. (One can also include Ayn Rand in this set, though she came to the United States from Russia long before World War II.) Ironically, given its current opposition to immigration, the American right was far more powered by foreign-born thinkers than the American left. Left-wing thinkers were typically the sons and daughters of immigrants, while conservative scholars and intellectuals tended to be immigrants themselves.

The paucity of the contribution of the émigré scholars to American liberalism is best illustrated by the fate of the Frankfurt school, often held up as one of the great intellectual movements of the twentieth century.[13] Max Horkheimer, its longtime director, never adjusted to living in Pacific Palisades, California, and returned to Germany in 1949. The polymath Theodor Adorno, perhaps the most brilliant of the group, did make a substantial contribution to American politics with *The Authoritarian Personality*, but he hated American culture, particularly jazz, and also returned to Germany after the war. Herbert Marcuse stayed in the United States, and while his writings had a significant impact on the New Left, he also left behind a form of naïve, even irresponsible radicalism. Among émigré thinkers as profound as these, one would think, a serious analysis of liberal democracy and its tensions would be forthcoming. It was not. The one great liberal thinker in the Frankfurt school tradition, Jürgen Habermas, never chose another country over his native Germany.

The situation was otherwise among American-born figures, not only Hofstadter, but Daniel Bell, Mary McCarthy, Dwight Macdonald, Diana and Lionel Trilling, Reinhold Niebuhr, Richard Wright, Daniel Patrick Moynihan, Louis Hartz, David Riesman, Seymour Martin Lipset, Nathan Glazer, and Arthur Schlesinger Jr. (John Kenneth Galbraith could be added to this list save for the fact that he was born in Canada.) They dealt directly with American life: in the case of Hofstadter and Schlesinger, its history; the Trillings its literature; Niebuhr its religious sensibility; Wright the complexities of race; Moynihan and Glazer the mysteries of ethnicity; and the other sociologists among them a Tocquevillian attempt to grasp American society as a whole. They were not deeply versed in the Western philosophical tradition, especially when compared to the dazzling erudition of scholars such as Arendt, but they also possessed something the émigrés did not have: a respect for concrete data, a concern for the everyday lives of ordinary citizens, and a facility with the English language that could at times produce gripping prose. These attributes drove their reflections on Joe McCarthy, and on what made his hour upon the stage possible. They pondered how their country, adhering to the longest-lasting written constitution in the world, could be so susceptible to a politics so utterly irresponsible. These thinkers, as Ira Katznelson wrote of them, along with political scientists such as David Truman, Robert A. Dahl, and Charles Lindblom, "were motivated to create political knowledge after the catastrophic and illiberal decades of devastation in order to discern means to guard and secure the best features of the West's patrimony."[14]

To say that we lack such thinkers in the age of Trump is to state the obvious. Our top universities, preoccupied with the training of specialized graduate students, no longer make much room for broadly educated public intellectuals along the lines of Riesman and Bell. Blogging is simply not the same thing as writing books or lengthy articles read by, and argued about, all the thinkers that matter, and tweeting, however useful for narcissists, is for intellectuals far more an insult than a challenge. Public commentators in America today lack the familiarity with the languages, literatures, and mores of other countries that came so naturally to the early postwar thinkers.

A deeply divided country has produced deeply divided thinkers, no longer able or willing to respect those on the other side. When McCarthy attacked, first-class intellectuals were there to respond. When Trump assumed power, although many newspaper columnists had much to say, academic voices could barely make themselves heard—or did not want to be heard.[15] It is not that we lacked a Tocqueville. We did not even have a (James) Bryce or a (Ralph) Lerner.

The decline of the public intellectual is a story told so often that it has received more than its share of debunkers. It is, however, unnecessary to enter that fruitless debate to understand why our age has so little rich commentary from broadly trained thinkers. The political scientist Daniel Drezner has drawn an important distinction between the public intellectuals of yesterday and the "thought leaders" of today.[16] Intellectuals may have been important for an era of books and public commentary, but thought leaders flourish in an age of TED Talks, PowerPoint, and global consulting. Rather than write broadly about many issues, they concentrate on one or two, hammering their message home in a series of books, many coauthored, and YouTube appearances. They seem always to be attending a conference somewhere and are often featured, dressed to the nines, in the latest issue of *The Economist* or the *New York Times Magazine*. (Think of the photogenic husband-wife team of Niall Ferguson and Ayaan Hirsi Ali.) Ideas have never been more present in American life. Whether they are deep ones is another question.

There are, for sure, a few contemporary academic thinkers with the range and power of the earlier generation: Michael Walzer, Amartya Sen, Alasdair McIntyre, Charles Taylor, and Martha Nussbaum would be on my list, and I surely have neglected other worthy figures. Still, the picture is quite different than it used to be. When *Foreign Policy* in 2009 published a list of the world's 100 leading public intellectuals, only two Americans—Noam Chomsky and Al Gore—were among them.[17] Chomsky, whatever one thinks of his views, and I disagree with most of them, is an intellectual of the old style. Gore is the quintessence of a thought leader. The charge that public intellectuals are in decline is a way of stating that thought leaders are in the ascendancy.

It is not, moreover, as if the intellectuals of earlier times have simply been forgotten; they have also been directly attacked. When the events of the 1960s radicalized so many of the young, one of their first targets was the generation of intellectuals that preceded them, a number of whom taught at universities, such as Columbia and Berkeley, that emerged as centers of student activism. Some, such as Glazer, who had assumed a public role during the Berkeley demonstrations of 1964, were attacked for what they did. Others, especially Hofstadter, were criticized for what they wrote. Where Hofstadter dismissed those adhering to right-wing ideologies and movements as "paranoid" or engaged in "pseudo" conservatism, younger scholars talked to the actual human beings who lived in such places as Orange County, California, and found that, as one wrote, "their right-wing ideology did evoke a distinctive worldview that provided a message of real meaning to its adherents."[18] Far from being first-rate critics who applied the ideas of great political thinkers to the American experience, the intellectuals of the 1940s and 1950s were now held to be "cold-war liberals," too attached to the American way of life to make any sense of it.[19] And as if all this were not damning enough, their group was composed overwhelmingly of white men, most of them of the same religion and ethnicity, putting them quite visibly at odds with America's current preoccupations with diversity.

At times the criticisms of the early postwar intellectuals went beyond the academic to the personal. Michael Kazin, a historian nearly always fair in his assessments, and the son of Alfred Kazin, one of the most accomplished of the New York intellectuals, nonetheless critiqued figures such as Bell and Glazer less for their actual arguments than for the fact that most of them were second-generation Jews struggling to find their place in a country they did not fully understand. "Having traveled in less than one generation from Union Square soapboxes to seminar rooms off Harvard Square and Morningside Heights," Kazin wrote, "liberal thinkers could never be secure." Their status in America being "fragile," their history was "simplistic." Kazin admirably defends ordinary folk, but this led him to dismiss McCarthy's critics: "On the basis of a handful of bombastic documents," he continued, "Bell and his fellow authors essentially conflated small farmers and wage earners who railed against private monopolies with right-wingers, often of comfortable means, who despised the New Deal state."[20] Whatever their flaws, Kazin believed, movements on behalf of social justice make the world a better place, a truth that the postwar political intellectuals, always wary of extremists, had, to their discredit, neglected.

Kazin admitted that these thinkers nonetheless found a "nugget of meaning" in the story they told. There also was, to be fair, a nugget of meaning in the criticisms he leveled against them. The early postwar intellectuals did make their share of mistakes. Their rightful hostility toward the Soviet Union translated itself into a rigid anti-communism that became, for some, an ideology unto itself. Seeing fascism in unexpected places, they exaggerated the dangers posed by both the student movements and the black protests of the 1960s. Equality for women was the furthest thing from their minds. Many of them, usually the first in their families to go to college, saw in affirmative action not a technique for promoting equality among the races, but a return to the era when Jews were kept out.[21] Indeed, most of them, with the exceptions of Richard Wright and Reinhold Niebuhr, seemed to have not all that much interest in the question of race at all; if anything, like Glazer and Moynihan, at least earlier in their careers, they took positions that ran against what many of the civil rights leaders of the time proposed. There is no gainsaying this neglect of race. The time in which they first began to write, the late 1940s and early 1950s, was especially ripe for a serious discussion of race; with considerable kicking and screaming the US Army had started to become racially integrated during World War II, and one of the major questions facing America at the end of the war was whether white southern politicians would return the country to the evils of segregation. Meanwhile, Gunnar Myrdal's *An American Dilemma* was published in 1944, and its findings demanded attention. For all these flaws, and perhaps for others they never committed, the early postwar liberals, like intellectuals everywhere, suffered a backlash.

Think, however, of what they got right. Who can doubt that in the years after McCarthy, the right in America adopted the language and style of populistic demagoguery? Richard Nixon relied upon a fear-mongering "Southern strategy" to sway a greater proportion of the white working class whatever the costs to black Americans; George Wallace adopted rhetoric even uglier than that of the senator from Wisconsin; Patrick Buchanan prophesied an unending culture war; Sarah Palin became a McCarthy without influence; Donald Trump became president; and a whole host of extreme right Republicans, including one actual Nazi in Illinois, decided to give running for office a try. There may have been an anti-democratic tinge to the writings of the early postwar intellectuals—more on that later—but they knew something about the dangers to democracy posed by charlatans claiming to be speaking in the name of the people. They may not have been conversant with Hegel and Heidegger, but otherwise their learning was prodigious, unmatched by most academics, alas very much including myself, today. For all their flaws, these thinkers stand redeemed today because they brought both the classical and the Enlightenment understandings of politics back to life and thereby offered a starting point for trying to understand why Americans, who profess to love democracy and freedom, elected as their president in 2016 a man and a party that seemed to respect neither.

Interpretations change: that is what makes them interpretations. Inevitably, therefore, what previously was seen as a settled matter becomes contested once again. This is very much the case with respect to the early postwar intellectuals. One could dismiss or even attack their positions so long as American politics showed some signs of stability. Alas, such complacency, given the right-wing demagoguery shaking both the world and this country, is no longer affordable. That is why, despite their occasional blind spots, it makes sense to return to what these intellectuals had to say.

How shall we describe the early American postwar thinkers politically? "Cold war liberals" will not do; they were indeed anti-Communist, but that is no mark against them, because it was the pro-Communists of their era who got so many things wrong. Nor am I happy with the term "centrist" liberals, for it tells us little of their actual positions.

Let me instead borrow from one of the most impressive among them, Reinhold Niebuhr, a favorite of the liberal Barack Obama, the conservative *New York Times* columnist David Brooks, and the nonpartisan former FBI director James Comey. (Not everyone agrees. Noam Chomsky said Niebuhr reflected "the shallowness and superficiality of the reigning intellectual culture," and that his ideas "are wonderful for war criminals." He's wrong.[22])

In the aftermath of two world wars and all their accompanying horrors, a number of left-wing activists, both religious and secular, found themselves captivated by the idea of world government. Niebuhr would have none of it. Nation-states, in his view, should use their power wisely rather than pretend they have no power to use, as world government would require. With advocates of global governance very much on his mind, Niebuhr insisted that "it would be the rightful function of a 'liberal' movement . . . to furnish the nation with mature counsel, assuming that liberalism . . . represents a measure of detachment from the shortsighted collective impulses of a community."[23] If his advice to America could be summarized in a few words, they would be reminiscent of 1 Corinthians 13–11: it is time to put away childish things. For this reason, Niebuhr is best called a mature liberal, and the political perspective developed by him and his peers can be characterized as mature liberalism.

For all of these thinkers, the McCarthy period and the subsequent emergence of the Goldwater right revealed a deep strain of immaturity in American political life. A mature society would cherish institutions that tried to preserve the best American traditions and practices. But American life in the 1950s had no patience for that. "Restless, mobile both geographically and socially, overwhelmingly middle-class in their aspirations, the American people have not given their loyalty to a national church or developed a traditionally oriented bar or clergy, or other institutions that have the character of national establishments," Hofstadter wrote.[24] McCarthy and the New Right filled in the gap left by the disappearance of the traditional ruling class. They grew so far and so fast because there was an insufficient number of grown-ups around to put a stop to their antics.

Maturity became the key idea that enabled these thinkers to

develop their critiques of American literature, popular culture, religion, and politics. One could substitute the word "mature" for "inner-directed" in David Riesman's *The Lonely Crowd*, for example, and not miss a beat. Arthur Schlesinger Jr. wrote in *The Vital Center* that "the beginnings of maturity in foreign policy lie in the understanding that a nation has certain unalterable interests which no government can abandon,"[25] and later found such maturity present in John F. Kennedy, despite his youth, while discovering it unfortunately lacking in Bill Clinton.[26] For Hofstadter, the problem with populist-style politics, embodied in William Jennings Bryan, was that Bryan never experienced what we call today a midlife crisis, in which one reflects on one's earlier life and grows from the experience: "The revolt of the youth against paternal authority, of the village agnostic against the faith of his tribe, of the artist against the stereotypes of the philistine life, of the socialist against the whole bourgeois community," Hofstadter wrote, "such experiences were not within his [Bryan's] ken."[27] Even if it is true that these thinkers did not fully grasp the depths of racism in America, the one who made it central to his writing, Richard Wright, also focused on the theme of maturity; in his memoir *Black Boy*, as well as in his contribution to the now-classic book *The God That Failed*, Wright discussed in often painful detail the conditions of his childhood in the South and the way he struggled with the Chicago Communist Party to resist being labeled a Negro or a Negro writer in order to assert his identity as a man.[28] (His life and writings, moreover, overlap with some of the leading African American writers of our own time, especially Ta-Nehisi Coates: Coates borrowed a line from Wright's poetry for the title of his book *Between the World and Me*, and his subsequent book on the Obama years argued that from a white perspective, President Obama was as mature a black leader as one could imagine, yet his moderation and quiet calm only fueled greater white anger toward him.[29]) Amazingly, Schlesinger was thirty-one when he published *The Vital Center*, Hofstadter was thirty-two when *The American Political Tradition* came out, Glazer was twenty-seven when his name appeared along with Riesman's on the cover of *The Lonely Crowd*, and Wright was fifteen when his first short story was published and twenty-four when he joined Chicago's John Reed Club, his introduction to the Communist Party. These were thinkers who discovered the importance of maturity at a very young age.

Other paeans to maturity were issued by the thinkers of this period. The Harvard political scientist Louis Hartz delivered one in *The Liberal Tradition in America* (1955). Hartz's ideas overlapped with those of the mature liberals; as the political scientist Paul Roazen wrote, "The tenor of Hartz's approach had its echoes in other writers of that time. David Riesman's *The Lonely Crowd* (1950), and his essays collected in *Individualism Reconsidered*, were written in a spirit akin to Hartz's; Lionel Trilling's *The Liberal Imagination* (1950) was a like-minded work with implications for social and political thought."[30] After a brilliant tour de force treatment of American thinkers from the New England Progressives to the Southern defenders of slavery, Hartz's own venture into these themes concluded with a brief reference to the McCarthy period: "This is the largest challenge the American liberal world has faced, and the payment for meeting it effectively is more than mere survival in an age of world turmoil. It holds out the hope of an inward enrichment of culture and perspective, a 'coming of age,' to use the term of the 'twenties again, which in its own right is worth fighting for."[31] "Coming of age" is as good a synonym for "maturity" as there is.

One need not be a social scientist to find the quality of maturity so valuable. An excellent definition of what a mature society requires was written by Lionel Trilling in an attempt to summarize Matthew Arnold's characterization of modernity. "A society," Trilling wrote, "is a modern society when it maintains a condition of repose, confidence, free activity of the mind, and tolerance for divergent views. A society is modern when it affords sufficient well-being for the conveniences of life and the development of taste. And, finally, a society is modern when its members are intellectually mature, by which Arnold means that they are willing to judge by reason, to observe facts in a critical spirit, and to search for the law of things."[32] Any society that even approximates such virtues would find Joseph McCarthy intolerable as a neighbor, let alone as a senator.

Permit me one final example of the importance these writers attached to maturity. A decade after McCarthy's downfall, Daniel Bell and Irving Kristol, generally known as the founder of neoconservatism, started a magazine, *The Public Interest.* While their effort is often taken as marking a change from left to right, the magazine also featured a transition from immaturity to maturity. As Kristol and Bell explained in their introduction to the magazine's first issue, the opposite of ideology was maturity:

> Unfortunately, there are always more adolescent minds than adolescents around. In the course of a conversation with the editors, one eminent man of letters remarked with an edge of scorn: "You appear to be publishing a middle-aged magazine for middle-aged readers." After thinking it over, we have decided that that is not such a bad description. Young people tend to be enchanted by glittering generalities; older people are inclined to remember rather than to think; middle-aged people, seasoned by life but still open to the future, do seem to us—in our middle years—to be the best of all political generations.[33]

At a time when the enthusiasm of the young was making its impact on America, Bell and Kristol wanted it to be known that they would speak for the grown-ups.

As all of these examples suggest, political maturity was the single most important idea that the midcentury liberals bequeathed to American thought. It was their antidote not only to Joe McCarthy but to all the demagogues that had appeared throughout American history before him. Their great hope was that the twin crises of depression and war would make it crystal clear to the American people that the time had come for them to get serious about politics. These thinkers chose to leave the ivory tower and contribute whatever they could to public understanding for one simple reason: just as a parent guides children to personal maturity, intellectuals can guide the general public to a greater sense of purpose about their collective lives. As a serious theologian, Reinhold Niebuhr found his vocation in doing just that. His colleagues, far more likely to be nonobservant even though raised Jewish, became secular public theologians, pondering, like the great rabbi Hillel, the great question of who is for whom. The 1950s was therefore a turning point for them. Because of the lessons learned from McCarthy, Americans, they hoped, would learn the dangers of demagoguery and elect more responsible leaders. Individuals experience growth spurts. Perhaps America could have one as well.

The key idea of mature liberalism was this: nearly two hundred years after its founding, America could not count on proclamations of its innocence to make its way in the world. The mature liberals, to use a term popular in its time, sought a middle way, but it was not only between left and right, as many have claimed, but between the naïve and the cynical. The problem of the left, in their view, was excessive innocence, while the right possessed an overabundance of world-weariness. Liberalism could be saved, these men and women believed, but only by a continual reinvention that would enable the American people to take account of a world that was becoming increasingly complex.

As will be made clear, maturity for these writers was not simply a stage we reach if we are lucky enough to hang around for sufficient years. It was instead a goal to be achieved by great effort so as to meet the world on its own terms. A mature people could help create the conditions for mature leadership, which in turn would enhance the maturity of the people. America, as Tocqueville wrote, was blessed with numerous advantages, especially the lack of a bloody revolution like that of France. But all those blessings would be lost if Americans failed to grow emotionally to keep pace with the growth of their industry and agriculture. The task of the mature liberals was to do everything in their power to help their fellow citizens realize and achieve their responsibilities. It is to their credit that they were willing to single out for criticism those who were not living up to the responsibilities of democratic citizenship. Democracy does not require that all its thinkers simply reaffirm common beliefs. It demands instead distance and discernment, the one to make judgments and the other to achieve them.

Because of their levelheadedness, the mature liberals were the last group of serious thinkers to consider politics, even or especially in its most practical and down-to-earth forms, a cause for celebration. To be sure, they were quite aware of the degenerate products of democratic politics: urban political machines, financial corruption, empty sloganeering. Yet they preferred the rough-and-tumble of political campaigns to the snotty, ineffective, upper class–based, and apolitical proposals offered by reformers such as the Progressives: politics for them was a noble enterprise even when its practitioners were not. The mature liberals, in other words, never held the contempt for politics and government so common in our own day. In their hard-nosed judgments, there remained strains of idealism, a sense that politics can and should represent the reality of who and what we really are. They certainly had their issues with the way our democracy works, but their only reason to call attention to democracy's flaws was to preserve it for those who benefit from its many advantages.

From the perspective of the second decade of the twenty-first century, the term "mature liberalism" will grate on many ears. This is clearly not a value-free term, like "New Deal liberalism," which simply describes, for praise or condemnation, what a person believes. Since maturity is generally preferable to immaturity, mature liberalism contains within it judgments. There, many critics will claim, lies the problem. Who are we intellectuals to decide what sets of people and ideas are mature and grown-up and which ones are childlike and naïve? Mature liberalism will be held to be offensive for the same reason that scholars have grown wary of using such terms as "developed countries" or "post-conventional morality"; it smacks of too much self-satisfaction. According to contemporary ways of thinking, we live in diverse times with multiple, and often conflicting, goals. The most ethical course is to let each have its proper voice. At root, mature liberalism will be held to suffer from an imperialist mentality, seeking to impose one way of living arbitrarily on others. In that, someone like Stanley Fish would argue, it is like all other liberalisms, claiming to be somewhere above the political fray but in actuality deep within it.[34]

Inevitably influenced by such criticisms, I rely on a term such as "maturity" with considerable trepidation: it definitely sounds tendentious to claim that the thinkers I admire so much were mature, implying that I must be as well, while far too many of the American people and the leaders they choose are not. But this is a risk one must take in writing about controversial subjects. I cannot ignore a truth that to me appears obvious: some leaders are simply better for the country than others, and what so often seems to characterize those who leave our society worse off are personality traits lacking in depth and perspective, needful of excessive flattery, focused almost entirely on themselves, and full of petulant anger when they do not get what they want. I do not know whether those who voted enthusiastically for Donald Trump consider him immature; they most likely do not. But at a time of great division in American life, the fact that critics from both sides of the political spectrum find Trump's narcissism unbearable suggests that there is indeed such a thing as political maturity, and that this president, as well as those who voted for him so enthusiastically, lack it.

We can see an example of the potential of mature liberalism in the first book to come to terms with the postwar American conservative movement, Daniel Bell's 1955 collection of essays, *The New American Right*.[35] The contributors included rising sociologists, such as Bell and Glazer, as well as Seymour Martin Lipset. David Riesman was already well known, having appeared on the cover of *Time* in 1954, and Talcott Parsons of Harvard was a sociology department unto himself. Hofstadter—on the verge of fame, as he won the first of his two Pulitzer Prizes, for *The Age of Reform*, that same year—contributed his thoughts on "pseudo conservative revolt."[36] *The New American Right* also included one avowed conservative, the poet and essayist Peter Viereck, a thoughtful man who had the misfortune to be the son of America's best-known Nazi.

What, they asked collectively, attracted people to the right? We learn little, they argued, by looking at the class positions of McCarthy's supporters. The more important factor was a subjective sense of having lost ground: the WASP elite to a rising meritocratic and professional upper middle class; small-town businessmen and farmers to city folk; and old-fashioned generals to technocrats with graduate degrees from MIT. Americans, Bell wrote, "have had an extraordinary talent for compromise in politics and extremism in morality." Frustrated by a society they no longer could recognize, "the dispossessed," as Bell called them in 1962, brought to America a sharper, more dangerous tone than previous movements of protest such as the Jacksonians and the Populists.[37] The radical right, in the view of these thinkers, was not just an elite reaction but a movement with significant support from below. This made it that much more powerful and that much more dangerous.

Even a summary as brief as this makes it clear that scholars such as Bell and Hofstadter were trying to replace the politics of class with a politics of status. One could not begin to understand the radical right, in their view, without acknowledging that the loss faced by those attracted to it was subjective and psychological as much as economic and measurable: one might easily compare wages across the years, but it was far more difficult to compare feelings of alienation. The trouble with an emphasis solely on class was its reduction of a complicated world to one thing and one thing only. A more mature perspective would not do that.

A sociologist not directly within the mature liberal circle, Joseph R. Gusfield, showed the way such a status-oriented perspective could contribute to an understanding of the larger social forces shaping American life. His book about Prohibitionism went well beyond economic and political explanations to demonstrate how those who felt their status slipping away mobilized their resentment into attacks on drinking.[38] Their hatred of alcohol, as well as their successful (for a time) effort to ban it, was not ethical so much as indignant; to them, the poor did not appear to be taking middle-class values seriously enough. For them, Prohibition was populism without people, and religion without a savior. Its goal was to protest the emergence of a culture that did not value hard work, family solidarity, and American patriotism as strongly as they thought it should. Gusfield's analysis, and especially the hostility of Prohibitionists toward immigrants, could not be more relevant to the cultural conflicts that have paved the way for the strong support quasi-populist candidates receive in middle America today.

Political economy, as these examples show, was simply too dry an approach for the mature liberals. Overall, they wanted their work to resonate more with the humanities than with the sciences, and the concept of status politics enabled this—though they would be criticized for abandoning Karl Marx in favor of Max Weber, a charge that was indisputably true. Yet they also characterized real human beings trying their best to deal with the complexities of modern life. Say this much for the radical right: those attracted to it were "once among the inarticulate masses," as Riesman and Glazer put it, but "are no longer silent."[39] In writing critically about radical rightists, the mature liberals were also giving them a voice. One need only to compare them to the all-too-relevant free market economists of the right or the stilted and now largely irrelevant Marxist-Leninist theories of the left to find heavily theoretical approaches to human behavior that leave actual human beings out of the picture. If these thinkers made a contribution to American intellectual history, it was to address what made America different from the rest of the world by relying on ideas the rest of the world brought to America.

Bell and the other mature liberals were not sure about the permanence of the new right-wing mood: Lipset thought it "extremely doubtful that the radical right will grow beyond the peak of 1953–54."[40] But Hofstadter proved to be more accurate when he wrote that "in a populistic political culture like ours, which seems to lack a responsible elite with political and moral autonomy, and in which it is possible to exploit the wildest currents of public sentiment for private purposes, it is at least conceivable that a highly organized, vocal, active, and well-financed minority could create a political climate in which the rational pursuit of our well-being and safety would become impossible."[41] Under the right conditions, we now know, that minority can become the majority, at least of the Electoral College.

Mature liberalism, having learned from the twentieth century's ugly history, would avoid the temptations of extremism of either the Stalinist or Hitlerite variety and instead energize what Arthur Schlesinger Jr. called the vital center. While these thinkers remained supportive of the reforms of the New Deal, they also believed, as the right turned increasingly radical in the aftermath of World War II, that the left ought to show a greater appreciation for an old-fashioned conservative sensibility: Hofstadter wrote that liberals "feel that we can better serve ourselves in the calculable future by holding onto what we have gained and learned, while trying to find some way out of the dreadful impasse of our polarized world, than by dismantling the social achievements of the past twenty years, abandoning all that is best in American traditions, and indulging in the costly pretense of repudiating what we should not and in fact cannot repudiate."[42] The 1950s revealed what Bell called "the exhaustion of political ideas." The truly important questions were where and how new ones could be found.

The critics of McCarthy offered some hints. A more mature liberalism, Bell wrote, would realize that there is more to life than economics and more to a good life than consumption, a point of view shared by Riesman, who was puzzled by abundance. Clearly rising wealth carried with it positive developments, not only greater comforts but more space in which to live and more alternatives from which young adults could choose. But beneath the surface dissatisfaction was evident, and it was not clear how social scientists should respond. "There are few channels, political or economic, for translating these as yet undefined shades of feeling into a program which could give us alternatives both to spending for defense and to spending for spending's sake," Riesman wrote in 1957.[43] Riesman feared not so much "total destruction" as "total meaninglessness." "It is my contention," he closed his essay by declaring, "that we may bring about the former because the latter inhibits our alternatives."

Riesman's ambiguous attitude toward abundance reinforced the point that for the postwar liberals, economics was never enough. Culture, by contrast, was. In a piece on his generation and its commitments, Bell pointed out that the most compelling problems of modern society were "essentially cultural and not political, and the problem of radical thought is to reconsider the relationship of culture to society." In doing so, Bell told his readers that his views were shaped by novelists such as James T. Farrell, Richard Wright, and John Dos Passos, as well as by philosophers such as Sidney Hook and all-purpose critics like Edmund Wilson. He further cited Niebuhr and Tillich as the kind of deep thinkers a more mature liberalism required.[44] *The Liberal Imagination*, by the Columbia University English professor Lionel Trilling, had a profound effect upon Bell, as did the University of Chicago sociologist Edward Shils, whose *The Torment of Secrecy* (1956) can be read as an additional chapter to *The New American Right*.[45] Economics frequently calls itself the queen of the social sciences. For these thinkers at that time, it was not.

Given their emphasis on culture, the mature liberals are best not characterized as progressives. It would certainly be nice if history amounted to one progressive victory over another. But the complexities of human nature disallow such a happy conclusion: no direct line to a better world can be found in the mature liberals' books and articles. His, Daniel Bell concluded, was a twice-born generation, and it found its wisdom in "pessimism, evil, tragedy, and despair."[46] Such pessimism is why Hofstadter, writing of the Goldwater campaign of 1964, cited the work of his colleague Fritz Stern on the turn to authoritarianism in German political thought before Hitler.[47] The unhappiness of these writers could become too extreme, certainly for my tastes. I prefer Hofstadter's more temperate language when he wrote in favor of a worldview "chastened by adversity, tempered by time, and modulated by a growing sense of reality" that would wean the reform impulse from "its sentimentalities and complacencies."[48] I can think of no more important contribution intellectuals can make today than to put sentimentality into its proper place: outside the realm of politics.

Do that, and right-wing reaction, especially in the form it took under Ronald Reagan, a master of fantasy with a penchant for delivering good news, will wither away.

Because I am speaking here of intellectuals, dissenters to the ideas of the mature liberals emerged almost as soon as the latter did. From the right, Irving Kristol defended McCarthy by claiming that, unlike radical leftists, the senator was at least vocally resolute in his anticommunism: neoconservatism, of which Kristol is generally held to be the godfather, thus emerged from the same stream as mature liberalism.[49] McCarthyism was just that kind of political phenomenon, one that gave the thinkers of the day little choice but to condemn or praise.

The mature liberals received their share of criticism from the left as well. The left's major thinker during the 1950s and 1960s was C. Wright Mills, the godfather of postwar academic leftism and a Columbia colleague of Hofstadter, Bell, Stern, and Trilling. Hofstadter and Mills, while radically different from each other in ideas, sensibility, dress, and means of transportation, "were also kindred spirits to the end," as Richard Gillam wrote, committed to the "critical ideal."[50] Curiously, however, Mills, who wrote about many things, never wrote anything about McCarthy (which did not preclude Shils, who had a strong taste for the polemical, from calling Mills "a sort of Joe McCarthy of sociology, full of wild accusations and gross inaccuracies, bullying manners, harsh words, and shifting grounds"[51]). It is as if McCarthy's messiness, his inconsistencies and irrationalities, interfered with Mills's preference for an ordered world of elite dominance in which the powerful always act to preserve and expand their power.

Mills's legacy is found today among social scientists who turn mature liberalism on its head by stressing the importance of political economy over culture: Daniel Bell may have emphasized culture so much because he perceived a common sociological bias against it, at least among left-wing writers for whom culture was epiphenomenal. Mills shared that view; for him, culture was a distraction, a kind of bread-and-circuses way to keep people's minds off the plans that the power elite had in store for them. We increasingly live, Mills believed, in a mass society that renders impossible the ideal that people can shape the cultural institutions that matter to them. Mass society was a valuable concept, as I will argue below, but in documenting this charge, Mills could easily border on the conspiratorial. "In addition to their enlarged and centralized means of administration, exploitation, and violence," he wrote, "the modern elite have placed within their grasp historically unique instruments of psychic management and manipulation, which include universal compulsory education as well as the media of mass communication."[52] Perhaps Shils was onto something: Mills might have avoided the issue of McCarthy because he could sound so much like him. No sense of irony would ever disturb Mills's certainty.

Bell was fond of drawing a distinction between the scholar, "who has a bounded field of knowledge, a tradition, and seeks to find a place in it, adding to the accumulated, tested knowledge as to a mosaic," and the intellectual, who "begins with *his* experience, *his* individual perceptions of the world, *his* privileges and deprivations, and judges the world by those sensibilities."[53] It is obvious why he did so. Not only was the grand sociological tradition of Max Weber and Émile Durkheim to which Bell appealed coming under attack from social science positivism, Trilling's literary eclecticism came to be viewed as old-fashioned belletrism rather than as serious scholarship. To cite just one example, René Wellek, another great émigré scholar, this time from Czechoslovakia, wrote that Trilling belongs "to critics of culture, in particular American culture, and is often concerned with questions of politics, pedagogy, psychology, and self-definition, which are only remotely related to literature."[54] This sounds like an exercise in academic boundary drawing designed to keep this class of intellectuals out. If so, it worked; Trilling never developed the reputation in academic circles that he did among fellow intellectuals.[55]

Mature liberalism, from start to finish was, in Bell's terms, not a scholarly but an intellectual project. That is why Hofstadter could borrow the term "paranoia" from more specialized clinical psychologists over the protests of many of them. It is also why, academically speaking, the contributors to *The New American Right* were such an odd lot. Bell and Glazer received their start in journalism, knew a thing or two about writing for the general public, and were granted doctorates based on previously published work. Glazer took eighteen years between his master's degree and his PhD. Riesman never received a doctorate at all, and Viereck taught at a four-year liberal arts college (Mount Holyoke) and not at a research university. These writers were not averse to numbers—Lipset's writing was full of them—but mindless number-crunching was not a methodological tool in their arsenal. It was extremely important for these thinkers to reach the general public—democracy, in their view, demanded as much. Fortunately, publishers at that time shared their goal: firms such as The Free Press and Basic Books, and the quality paperback revolution launched by Jason Epstein first at Doubleday and then Random House, brought erudite academic writers, especially the ones I have been discussing, to generally educated readers. By the rules of contemporary academic history, one must never call an earlier period a golden age. With respect to the early postwar intellectuals, I have a hard time resisting.

Five years after *The New American Right* was published, John F. Kennedy was elected president, and he was open not only to ideas in general but to the specific ideas of the participants in the debate over McCarthy: Schlesinger became his close adviser, and Bell's concept of the end of ideology provided the substance of Kennedy's 1962 Yale commencement address.[56] Kennedy, moreover, for all his flaws as a politician, especially in the area of civil rights, evoked a language of service and seriousness of purpose that the mature liberals could, and did, admire; as Schlesinger put it, in a near-perfect summary of the virtues of mature liberalism, Kennedy's disposition was "objective, practical, ironic, skeptical, unfettered, and insatiable."[57] It seemed, however briefly, that mature liberalism would gain and hold time in the limelight.

All that went into abeyance with Kennedy's assassination, for Lyndon Johnson preferred to hang out with other kinds of people. (His favorite intellectual/scholar was Eric F. Goldman of Princeton, a historian whose name has been all but forgotten.[58]) Kennedy's Yale speech proved to be the high point of cooperation between intellectuals and politicians. Mature liberalism, it turned out, lacked the sense of rage appropriate to the developing Vietnam War and America's continued inability to deal with the issue of race. The end of ideology, in addition, seemed like an absurd idea when Communists were in power in Cuba and the Soviet Union, and the student rebels, myself included, found wisdom in the Marxist classics. Under conditions of such turmoil, mature liberalism became senescent: it found itself transformed into a sclerotic centrism, resting on its laurels and no longer inspiring.

The United States is a very different country now than it was in the 1940s and 1950s—more diverse, more urban, better educated, somewhat more racially integrated, indeed better off in general. But this does not mean that this country is immune from demagogic appeals. Previous populists such as William Jennings Bryan or Huey Long might have attacked the wealthy, while contemporary conservative populists lavish them with tax breaks. But the political immaturity underneath is very much the same, if not worse. A sustained redistribution of income from the poorest to the wealthiest, along with seemingly uncontrollable globalizing forces, has left behind pockets of the white working class so filled with resentment that it was only a matter of time before they made an impact on American democracy. One can characterize this phenomenon any way one wishes. For me, Daniel Bell's term "the dispossessed" is as good as it gets.

This, I grant, is not a very flattering term. Writing about right-wing Republicans in Orange County, Lisa McGirr comments: "To label this group as America's 'dispossessed,' . . . presents a distorted and inaccurate portrait and does not accord with these individuals' sense of themselves or their worldview."[59] Yet the terms used by Bell and his colleagues strike me as remarkably useful for Trump voters, those who feel so strongly that their country has been taken away from them because some of its leaders look different than them. Confirmation for this view can be found in the writings of the journalist most familiar with social science research: Thomas Byrne Edsall. (Edsall's father-in-law was another émigré from Czechoslovakia, the extremely distinguished political scientist Karl Deutsch.) "These are men and women," Edsall wrote about Trump voters in the aftermath of the 2016 election, "who are, in the main, still working, still attending church, still members of functioning families, but who often live in communities where neighbors, relatives, friends and children have been caught up in disordered lives. The worry that this disorder has become contagious—that decent working or middle class lives can unravel quickly—stalks many voters, particularly in communities where jobs, industries, and a whole way of life have slowly receded, the cumulating effect of which can feel like a sudden blow."[60] People secure in their status and democratic in their sensibilities do not need demagogues to lead them. People who feel threatened by their loss of status do. If they relied more on themselves than the hysterical admonitions of their would-be politicians—very much like David Riesman's "inner-directed people"—they would be in a better position to know what was best for them and their country.

The early postwar liberals, frightened by the success of McCarthy and the rise of the radical right, were more aware than most of the extent to which demagogic leaders lacked the maturity required to be effective leaders of their country. Their influence has not completely disappeared from American politics. In 2009, for example, Barack Obama, as we have seen, an avid reader of Reinhold Niebuhr, reminded Americans in his first inaugural address that "the time has come to put away childish things."[61] Donald Trump's single determination as president has been to repudiate everything his predecessor said and did, evidently including taking the childish things back out of the closet and playing with them so vividly on the public stage. Insightful as they were, the early postwar liberals could never have imagined anything like the petulant child who now occupies the Oval Office. It is our curse, but perhaps also our blessing, that we have no choice but to see through the glass of American politics darkly.

2

DEMOCRACY'S DEMAGOGUE

Rooted in the political philosophy of ancient Greece and Rome, the political education of America's founders was filled with stories involving classic demagogues. One of the most notorious was Cleon, an Athenian general who, in the words of Michael Signer, "toppled a revered statesman, took over the Athenian government, came within a hair of executing a powerful playwright who challenged him, attempted the mass murder of the inhabitants of a vanquished island, launched reckless military expeditions, and brought Athens into a war that would ultimately defeat its democracy for a time."[1] (Donald Trump has a long way to go if he wants to hold the world record in demagoguery.) Aristotle, Thucydides, and Aristophanes all wrote about Cleon, none favorably. If you are trying to establish a democracy, as America's founders were trying to do, his was a name you never forgot.

All of these thinkers, however much they understood tyranny, were unable to ponder the potential dangers of populism, since, technically speaking, no such thing could exist in their day. Populism, as its name implies, presumes the existence of a people, that is, a population that actively chooses its leaders. (Why appeal to them if they have no role in governance?) Not only that, but the people must be differentiated into two or more groups so that the populist can play one group off the others.[2] It is true that the later stages of the Roman republic witnessed a conflict between the more conservative *optimates*, whose support lay with the patricians, and those known as the *populares*, who acted more in the interests of the plebeians. But the leaders of both groups were upper class, and neither sought to fundamentally transform a political system so beneficial to them and their families. There was no Greek or Roman William Jennings Bryan, let alone a Donald Trump. Nor was there such a figure for Publius to warn about in the Federalist Papers.

The populist is democracy's demagogue. He comes into being with the expansion of suffrage, and if need be, he will expand suffrage even further to gain additional support. The greater the amount of democracy, the greater the potential of populism. With the collapse of communism and the rise of Third World self-determination, populism, given more room to flourish, has now emerged as one of the major political forces not only in the United States and Europe, but also in much of the rest of the world.

The contemporary scope of populism is indeed remarkable. Leaders such as Hugo Chávez of Venezuela, Evo Morales of Bolivia, and Viktor Orbán of Hungary have all been described as populists. Populist parties have shown powerful electoral strength in well-established, and generally liberal, European democracies, such as Holland, Denmark, and Finland. Great Britain's vote to leave the European Union, known as Brexit, is widely viewed as populist. No wonder there is talk today of a "populist explosion," a breakout of mass discontent around the globe, marked by hostility toward entrenched elites whose policies—economic globalization, a welcoming attitude toward immigration, and tolerance of a widening gap between rich and poor—are said to inflict additional pain on masses of people who already lead lives marked by increasingly unquiet desperation.[3] The populist wave promises to be quite powerful. It seemed to peak with the failure of Marine Le Pen to even come close to winning the French presidency in May 2017. But that was followed by the success of the far-right Alternative for Germany later in that year and then the 2018 Italian elections, in which populists and nationalists managed to win a majority of the votes.

Given populism's frequency, political scientists have been searching for proper definitions that can best describe what it is. I offer this one because it seems to capture what makes populism distinctive from other political movements and expressions. The five most common characteristics of populism can be summarized as follows. (1) The populist leader divides society into at least two groups or classes: those who express its ethnic, racial, religious, or ideological identity in its purest form and those who remain, most likely forever, outsiders because of who they are, what they believe, or both. (2) In full charismatic fashion, the populist leader takes up the case of the "true" members of the society and offers an explanation, usually very simplified, of why they feel alienated. (3) This alienation is inevitably attributed to people who are in one or another way different from the majority, eventually leading populists to flirt with racism, xenophobia, or both. (4) The populist proclivity is anti-institutional, bypassing, if possible, organized political parties and established interest groups in favor of rallying support directly from followers. (5) The fuel that makes the populist car run is distrust: there is something radically amiss about all existing institutions, and only the populist as hero can fix it.

One item is conspicuously missing from my definition: what the populist leader and his or her followers actually believe. That is because, with populism, form trumps content. This may at first seem absurd because contrasting programs generally underlie most political struggles, and it clearly matters whether a candidate is progressive or reactionary. But there are two major reasons why this approach nonetheless makes sense. One is that populism appears in many ideological guises, even when led by the same individual, and if all of these movements are to be compared, it must be on the basis of something other than content. The other is that emphasizing populism's form is the best way to understand the dangers it poses to democracy, because populism offers such a vivid example of the most pronounced form that political immaturity takes in the contemporary world.

The populism so widespread today certainly crosses the ideological spectrum. In much of Latin America, populism is generally viewed as a movement of the left pressing for egalitarian goals. Venezuela's Chávez, an authoritarian demagogue through and through, pushed for radical policies such as nationalization of the oil companies and comprehensive land reform. Europe as well has witnessed left-wing populist movements, such as Spain's Podemos and Greece's Syriza. The ideas of the late Argentinean Ernesto Laclau, at one time a writer of dense Marxist prose of the poststructuralist variety, appealed to activists in both countries. Laclau speaks of the construction of the term "the people" as a revolutionary breakthrough, much as Marx viewed the formation of the proletariat, because, in the act of making the people a group in and for itself, "universal-equivalent identifications prevail over sectorial ones."[4] It was comforting for him and his followers to believe that there will always be a force pushing for revolution, even if it is now not the ever-smaller proletariat but the more amorphous people.

Even the most cursory glance at recent experience suggests that there is also populism of the right; nearly all the remaining European experiments with populism are of this nature. Right-wing populism feeds off nationalism and lingers on resentment, or, to use the French term, *ressentiment*. Its programs advocate cutting taxes and small government. It sells itself in election campaigns as the alternative to the further integration of Europe and all the regulations and taxation associated with it. Its anti-Muslim bias closely resembles the anti-Semitism that plagued Europe for centuries. European populism can turn so ugly that at least one writer, the Dutch philosopher Rob Riemen, suggests that it really ought to be called fascism.[5] Populism of the right joins the British vote for Brexit with the American vote for Trump: it would be difficult to associate the leaders of these two campaigns with anything that smacks of leftism. Indeed, Trump himself, for all his political inexperience and lack of historical knowledge, campaigned in 2016 as a populist very much in the classic tradition.[6]

What, then, connects those who wish to see banks nationalized and those who call for an end to bank regulations? Does it make any sense to link under the same term those who promise more to the poor and those who give more to the rich? The key to understanding populism is that, yes, such lumping together makes sense. For one thing, populism of the right shares one important feature with populism of the left: both treat liberalism with disdain.

The left-wing contempt for liberalism is given expressive treatment in the writings of bloggers such as Glenn Greenwald and Cory Doctorow. Greenwald takes a typical "enemy of my friend" approach. Since Trump's populism was an attack on the 'bipartisan Washington consensus" that has caused so much damage in its corporatist domestic policies and neo-imperial foreign ones, Trump, he argues, despite his nativism and right-wing sentiments, is nonetheless a force for progress.[7] Doctorow, a Canadian blogger and science-fiction writer, goes one step further in accounting for Trump's popularity: "As neoliberalism and its handmaiden, corruption, have swept the globe, making the rich richer, the poor poorer, and everyone in the middle more precarious; as elites demonized and dismissed the left-behinds who said something was wrong; as the social instability of inequality has been countered with increasingly invasive domestic 'war on terror' policing, millions of people are ready to revolt, and will support anyone who promises no more business as usual."[8] All this was a backhand way of preferring Donald Trump to Hillary Clinton. To many Trump supporters, Clinton was a traitor to her country. To the populist left, she was a traitor to her cause. Her defeat in 2016 was a good thing, because, in discrediting neoliberalism, she has prepared the way for populism.

Those on the right detest liberalism for a different reason: its sympathy for illegal immigrants and reluctance to expand police forces, as well as its archaic insistence on due process of law and individual rights. Liberalism, to them, free-associates with weakness, women, and waste: it refuses to confront its enemies, values the softer virtues such as compassion, and spends inordinately on programs motivated by a compassion they believe is misplaced. (No wonder so many populist parties in Europe have male leaders.[9]) Nor do populists admire the ideology of that narrow and distorted form of liberalism called libertarianism. Stephen K. Bannon, President Trump's former chief strategist, once said that libertarians "are not living in the real world"—and they tend not to like him in turn.[10] In their view, Bannon relies too much on the state, primarily to keep order, to be an advocate of freedom, including economic freedom.

There does exist a debate as to whether Bannon, who knew enough political philosophy to drop names, was an in-depth reader or just an above-average hustler. Bannon may be gone from playing any major role in American politics—or maybe he will return to prominence in the future—but it is still unusual to see a powerful figure cite obscure figures known for their contempt toward liberalism, none more important than the Italian Fascist Julius Evola, who combined traditional European conservative themes with the mysterious and the occult appeals of Eastern religion. The 2016 election, furthermore, was accompanied by a serious effort at intellectual theorizing by one Publius Decius Mus, who wrote an influential article called "The Flight 93 Election," the theme of which was "Charge the cockpit or you die."[11] The author was quickly identified as Michael Anton, who was later appointed to a position on Trump's National Security Council. Anton, who resigned in 2018, believes that America's days are numbered—indeed, that the election of Hillary Clinton would have done the country in—and prone to talk about how liberalism leads directly to decadence. "I'm a huge admirer," Bannon told an interviewer. "I think Michael is one of the most significant intellects in this nationalist movement."[12]

This mutual contempt from both ends of the political spectrum is dangerous to the health of liberal democracy. Even in well-established political systems, democracy is always fragile. Populism, wherever it appears, is always blunt. Ignore populist demands and the anger that fuels it only increases, at least until it burns out. Accept the populist as normal, and the procedural practices that make liberal democracy possible—the rule of law, compromise and negotiation, pluralism, and respect for the Constitution—begin to atrophy. Populism presents democracy with a "damned if you do and damned if you don't" choice. It is therefore essential to look beyond populism's leftist content if you are leftist, and its rightist content if you are rightist. Alas, this is rarely done. Because having the people on your side is too advantageous to resist, populism yields all too often to opportunism: to the left, populism promises equality; to the right, popularity. Nonetheless, populism is the fool's gold of political ambition, always tempting to use, but always costly to apply. And we all, whatever our politics, pay the same price when populism succeeds, reducing the complexity of the events we face to the lowest level of understanding.

The United States was one of two countries that invented populism, the other being Russia and its Narodniks, middle-class reformers trying to awaken the peasants from their political slumber. While others had written about populism before them—John Hicks's *The Populist Revolt* appeared in 1931[13]—the mature liberals of the early post–World War II period were the first to theorize about American populism, to think seriously about why it appeared, and to consider what its appearance foreshadowed. While much has been written since, including a number of criticisms of what they wrote, the approach they developed still offers the most useful tool in explaining populism's contemporary attractions. Their most important contribution was this: unimpressed with populism's presumed love of the people, or even the love of the people in return, they understood that populism, an exceptionally dangerous form of political immaturity, was best avoided, no matter what its content.

The Populist Party made its first appearance on the American scene in 1892, when it nominated James K. Weaver, a former congressman from Iowa, for president. In its early years, the movement attracted a colorful group of followers, none more so than Ignatius Donnelly, a progressive Minnesota politician who wrote books about the fate of the mythical city Atlantis and the "true" author of Shakespeare's plays, Francis Bacon. "A vast conspiracy against mankind has been organized on two continents and is rapidly taking possession of the world," Donnelly told those who had met to nominate Weaver.[14] The targets of these conspirators were ordinary men and women, the farmers, and even, at times, the urban workers who produced the country's wealth. All those manipulated by diabolic Mammon needed to join together, he and other populists believed, to reclaim the moral virtues of the commonwealth. For this reason the platform agreed to by the first Populist Party presidential candidate included such provisions as the unlimited coinage of gold and silver as well as shorter days for workers. Populism began with a many-pronged set of proposals. As Michael Kazin points out, it offered "an agenda neither of the two parties would support" and "it clearly showed a desire to move away from the monistic nostrums that had gripped the competing battalions of reform for a generation."[15]

Soon merging with the Democrats, populism became strongly identified with William Jennings Bryan, a three-time presidential candidate from Nebraska. As he made clear in his famous "Cross of Gold" speech in 1896, one of the most impressive American political speeches ever delivered, Bryan spoke on behalf of "those hearty pioneers who braved all the dangers of the wilderness, who have made the desert to blossom as the rose—those pioneers away out there, rearing their children near to nature's heart, where they can mingle their voices with the voices of the birds—out there where they have erected schoolhouses for the education of their children and churches where they praise their Creator, and the cemeteries where sleep the ashes of their dead."[16] Rallying to their cause, Bryan appeared to be one in a long series of American reformers trying to promote greater equality and respect for the ordinary American, standing, as he did, more than midway between Andrew Jackson and Franklin Roosevelt. Look for the equivalent of that Bryan today, and one might settle on Bernie Sanders, a secular Jew from Brooklyn who nearly won the Democratic presidential nomination in 2016—a man as far from Bryan, culturally and ethnically, as possible. We are told by his sympathetic biographer that Bryan remained unappreciated by the left, which "largely ignored how central he had been to many of the issues for which it continued to struggle—the rights of labor and women, the regulation of big business, the reform of campaign finance, progressive taxation, anti-militarism, and more."[17] Perhaps the Sanders campaign of 2016 brought that neglect to an end.

Because farmers in the United States were not just embattled, but also reflected the agrarian virtues long associated with their country, Bryan spoke mainly to the plain folk, nearly all of them white and similar in the way they worshipped their God. That may be why he opted to join the prosecution of John Scopes, a Tennessee teacher who insisted on teaching the theory of evolution even though such a practice was deemed illegal by the state legislature. This Bryan is remembered as an advocate of "the old time religion." Although not permitted to deliver his closing speech in the Scopes trial, it was nonetheless published posthumously, and in it Bryan made clear that he had appeared at the trial as a messenger from the Lord; the trial presented "a choice between God and Baal" and served "as a renewal of the issue in Pilate's court."[18] From this Bryan one can draw a straight line to Tony Perkins, Ralph Reed, and others in the forefront of today's religious right; indeed, Reed once praised Bryan as "the most consequential evangelical politician of the twentieth century."[19] Today, this Bryan would be invited to speak at the Conservative Political Action Conference before offering his blessings on the National Day of Prayer.

So which Bryan is it: the principled liberal who resigned as Woodrow Wilson's secretary of state to protest war fever or the God-cloaked seller of nostrums as worthless as late-night television ads for vegetable choppers? Richard Hofstadter had no doubt. In 1948, he published *The American Political Tradition and the Men Who Made It.* Everyone was grist for this gifted young historian's iconoclastic mill: Jefferson was as much an aristocrat as a democrat, John C. Calhoun was the "Marx of the Master Class," and Bryan, poor Bryan, was a preacher of "political primitivism" whose "heart was filled with simple emotions" while "his mind was stocked with equally simple ideas."[20] To a reader accustomed to bloodless academic history, Hofstadter's language was unabashed, if not shocking. "Bryan decayed rapidly during his closing years. The postwar era found him identified with some of the worst tendencies in American life—prohibition, the crusade against evolution, real-estate speculation, and the Klan. . . . Fat, balding, in wrinkled clothes, taxed by the heat, bereft of the splendid voice that had made him famous, he was unequal to the merciless heckling from the galleries."[21] Hofstadter sought nothing less than to upset nearly everyone's conventional wisdom about how American history developed, and toppling Bryan from his progressive throne was an important step in this process.

Although numerous distinguished historians would criticize Hofstadter's approach to populism,[22] his views significantly shaped how the mature liberals of the early postwar period understood Joe McCarthy and the emerging conservative moment in America. "The radical right of the early 1960s," wrote Daniel Bell, "is in no way different from the Populists of the 1890s."[23] As he often did, Seymour Martin Lipset fleshed out Bell's point with numbers. Relying on surveys, Lipset showed that McCarthy's support did not come from traditionally Republican big businessmen but from small business owners who might, under other conditions, have voted for the left.[24] For David Riesman and Nathan Glazer, the key supporters of McCarthy lay among the "new underprivileged rich," those who lived in such states as Texas and California and were making money hand over fist. Unable to match the East Coast elite in class and breeding, these conservative voters were naturally attracted to a politician who denounced the Ivy League establishment as readily as he did Communist activists. "Senator McCarthy, with his gruff charm and Populist roots, seems made to order for such men," they wrote.[25]

In 1957, Victor Ferkiss, a political scientist, argued that populism and fascism arose from the same roots, had similar ideas, and attracted the same kind of people.[26] It was a controversial thesis, and it is worth emphasizing that the mature liberals did not go as far. They used but did not overuse terms such as fascism, and in any case Ferkiss did not do a very good job of establishing links between the two political phenomena. But the mature liberals nonetheless agreed that populism was bad for democracy. It is therefore worth asking what precisely it was about populism that sent up so many warning flags to these thinkers. I see three indications of danger: extremism, simplification, and irresponsibility.

"McCarthy," Lipset wrote, "had no party, not even an organization, but for a few years he ranged the American political scene denouncing the forces of the left—the New Deal Democrats—as traitors or the accomplices of traitors, and at the same time insisted that the bulk of the traitors were nurtured by the traditional enemy of populism, the

Eastern upper class." The anxiety that fed the radical right was free-floating, Lipset believed; it lacked a home in any institution that might have moderated it. This did not prevent William Jennings Bryan from joining the Democrats, running for president under their banner, and proudly identifying with the party. But nonetheless the anxiety that fed the radical right, lacking roots, could pop up anywhere, premised on a rejection of whatever forces were holding it down. "A stable democracy," Lipset wrote, "requires relatively moderate tension among its contending political forces." The Populists violated this principle by appealing to only one, rather homogenous group and for that reason alone were not democracy's friend. "Wherever the social structure operates so as to isolate *naturally* individuals or groups with the same political outlook from contact with those who hold different views," Lipset continued, "the isolated individuals or groups tend to back political extremists."[27]

Interestingly enough, defenders of populism, such as Ernesto Laclau, agreed with this formulation. Against Bryan's appeals to the people as a whole, Mark Hanna, William McKinley's adviser, had created the slogan of a "progressive society." Laclau did not view the term favorably. Hanna, he wrote, envisions a society in which "there is no longer any appeal to a homogenous, undifferentiated mass, but to the organic, orderly development of a society, each of whose members had a precisely defined place, and whose centre was an elite identified with American values."[28] Democracy creates distinctions. Populism abolishes them. Freed from organizational ties, the populist mass is freed from the confinements of the political center. It was precisely the persistence of that "homogenous, undifferentiated mass" that Laclau viewed as an opening for populism. His enemies were pluralism, organized political parties, and moderation.

It is characteristic of our times that the term "extremism" is less and less used in American politics. (It remains very popular in talking about radical Islam, however.[29]) Perhaps that is because "extremism" is something of an empty term, devoid of any actual content, like an adjective divorced from a noun to modify. Yet at the time the mature liberals wrote, something called extremism did exist and did appear dangerous; there had been a radical left and a radical right, and they both located themselves off the usual, and admittedly narrow, political spectrum. In the face of both, there is no doubting that the mature liberals were ideologists of the center: they wished more for stability than for radical change.

Today, however, in the United States, the radical left is no longer much of a force, while ideas within the far right—a freedom to own and use arms so broadly defined that it would have been unrecognizable earlier in US history, for example, or religious freedom redefined to *favor* churches rather than to limit their reach—have become the stuff of ordinary party politics. When the Goldwater platform of 1964 is to the *left* of the Republicans' 2016 platform—the earlier platform was filled with abstract generalities, although it did promise, unlike the candidate running on it, "a strong and sound system of Social Security, with improved benefits to our people"[30]—what more can be said about extremism, other than it can no longer be found just at the extremes?

From the Great Depression until the McCarthy period, the first target against which the mature liberals devoted their fire was the left: nearly all of these thinkers had joined Socialist parties or movements during their youth, and they found themselves appalled by the idea of a "popular front" in which liberals would join with Communists to protest the status quo. In 1947, Americans for Democratic Action was founded to be both liberal and anti-Communist; Reinhold Niebuhr and Arthur Schlesinger were active in the formation. Others in their circle became enthusiasts for the young mayor of Minneapolis, Hubert Humphrey, who was running for the Senate and spoke as a strong advocate for civil rights at the 1948 Democratic convention, but who had also fought Communists for control of his state's Farmer-Labor Party. It is, of course, possible to view the mature liberals as incipient cold warriors; their anti-Communism was that strong. But they believed that the presence of a man sympathetic to the Communists on the 1948 presidential ballot was a cause for concern. Former agriculture secretary Henry Wallace, who ran for president in 1948 on the Communist-influenced Progressive Party ticket, was exactly the kind of politician they distrusted, as left-wing in politics as he was unsophisticated in his person.

McCarthy did a lot to change all this; his rise to power in the 1950s reminded liberals that similar forms of right-wing populism were taking shape simultaneously outside the United States. In France, Pierre Poujade, previously a stationery-store owner, led an anti-tax protest during the 1950s that can be considered that country's first experience with right-wing populism: Poujade, it has been said, is the "grandfather" of today's right-wing extremist Marine Le Pen.[31] The same period witnessed the first two presidencies of the Argentine strongman Juan Perón. Perón attracted followers from both the right and the left, including labor union members, but his authoritarianism, overt nationalism, and sympathy toward the military, at least according to Lipset, located him firmly in the camp of fascism, even though in his case it was left-wing. Consideration of extremism was important to these thinkers because, at the time they wrote, extremism was plentiful. Radical movements could destabilize democracy, they believed, because the ground away from the center was less likely to hold. It was not just ideological attraction that drew these thinkers to the middle way, in other words, but genuine concern over how much pressure liberal democracy could withstand. The era of totalitarianism, genocide, and world conquest, after all, had only recently ended.

Political matters have certainly changed since then. The mature liberals worried about the radical right influencing elections, not winning them, and the idea that yesterday's member of the John Birch Society would be today's Republican congressman from just about anywhere in the South would have shocked them. We therefore must answer a question they were able to avoid: is extremism more of a danger when outside or inside the government?

As political scientists are wont to say, it depends. Take, for example, Italy, where, in the immediate postwar period, the threat to liberal democracy, once fascism was defeated, seemed to come from the left. (Italy was important to the mature liberals because of their friendships with two Italian writers, Ignazio Silone, who shared their anticommunism, and Nicola Chiaromonte, who became a close friend of the writer Mary McCarthy and figured in her roman à clef, *The Oasis*.) In 1948, in elections to choose the first postwar parliament, Italy's Christian Democrats defeated a popular front coalition between the Socialists and the Communists. Both of the latter parties were viewed as extremist, certainly by the CIA, which played an important role in helping the Christian Democrats win. Yet that money might not have been well spent. The Italian Socialist leader Pietro Nenni broke with the Communists in 1956 after the Soviet invasion of Hungary, and by the 1960s, the Communists themselves appeared to be quite moderate in comparison to New Left movements such as the Red Brigades. Power and time, it seems, do moderate. If it happened in Italy, could it happen in the United States?

The answer appears to be no. America's threat was from the right rather than the left, and that made all the difference. Extremists of the right have been able to take control of the Republican Party, and we can say, pretty much for certain, that in the United States holding power can increase ideological extremism. If one of the major problems with the radical right was, as Hofstadter maintained, its anti-intellectualism, there is no reason why holding power will change that, as the Trump presidency, led by a man who makes Hofstadter's examples of anti-intellectualism seem like pointy-headed supporters of Adlai Stevenson, clearly demonstrates. Attack Hofstadter all you want for his use of the term "paranoia," but those who see conspiracies everywhere, once they obtain a wider view from assuming office, are likely to see more of them. In theory, holding power should introduce realism into the conduct of foreign policy, undermining the more naïve isolationism attractive to those out of power, but that same power can go to a leader's head, making him and his country appear immune to the time-tested teachings of international relations.

There was the time when institutions such as the undemocratic US Senate and Electoral College were considered moderators of extremism, especially of the majoritarian form. Now the American political system contains numerous extremism enhancers, practices, and institutions designed to increase the amount of extremism year after year. The clearest example involves the judiciary. The postwar intellectuals were not preoccupied, as we are, with the Supreme Court. Perhaps the single most important change in US politics since they wrote has been the transition of the court to a ringside seat in the culture war. In the past, justices did, at times, moderate, or even change, their positions, much to the chagrin of the presidents who appointed them. These days, active steps are taken at every stage in the appointment process, from generating a shortlist to testifying before Congress, to guaranteeing, as much as possible, that no moderation will ever take place. Along the same lines, previous presidents did not pay particular attention to the age of a potential judge; if anything, judges were believed to need the wisdom of more advanced years. Now presidents seek the youngest possible judges to secure longer fidelity to ideological principles. It cannot be all that surprising that the most undemocratic of the three branches of government acts the most undemocratically. Its isolation from day-to-day politics facilitates its role as an incubator of extremism.

It is, moreover, not just the courts—majorities in Congress will do what they have to do to keep their extremism intact. Politicians have learned the art of gerrymandering district boundaries to limit two-party competition for seats. Informal agreements and mutual trust once presented shortcuts to leaders seeking bipartisan cooperation but are now used to increase ideological gridlock. When McCarthy dominated American politics, sufficient means of restraining his appeal, such as critical actions undertaken by his fellow Republicans, remained. But now, with partisanship considered so much more important than ideology, or even stability, or even patriotism, populistic appeals are far more dangerous than they were in the 1950s. This does not mean that right-wing populists get their way. The inability of the right to obtain the repeal of Obamacare while holding both houses of Congress in the first year of the Trump administration has surprised everyone, the right included. And even when the extreme right did manage to pass legislation, such as a 2017 tax policy that worked overwhelmingly to benefit the already rich, it did so by the narrowest of margins.

In their own way, the mature liberals understood the possibility of extremism becoming a fixture of government. Bell, I believe, got it right when he wrote:

> Something new has been happening in American life. It is not the rancor of the radical right, for rancor has been a recurrent aspect of the American political temper. Nor is it just the casting of suspicions or the conspiracy theory of politics, elements of which have streaked American life in the past. What is new, and this is why the problem assumes importance far beyond the question of the fight for control of a party, is the ideology of this movement—its readiness to jettison constitutional processes and to suspend liberties, to condone Communist methods in the fighting of Communism.[32]

Bell's fears of right-wing extremism resonate today. We now have right-wingers who borrow from left-wing intellectuals, whether they be Saul Alinsky or V. I. Lenin, to justify their activism. I doubt that these odd couplings would have surprised the mature liberals.

"We do not live 'at extremes,'" Bell wrote. "That is why, perhaps, we have avoided some of the extreme ideological conflicts that wrecked Europe."[33] He may have been correct for his time, but prophetic these words are not. We do now live at a time of extremes, and we may even have a thing or two to tell Europe about its dangers. All the more reason, then, to follow the advice of the mature liberals. We should not "normalize" extremist politicians just because they hold office. We should never hope for victories of the radical right as a way of advancing the agenda of the radical left. And we should never take our democracy for granted: we have to be on constant alert, especially when candidates or the media start throwing around words such as "populist" too loosely. Otherwise, the people are likely to support leaders who, in the name of the people, serve them badly.

To paraphrase the German political scientist Ralf Dahrendorf, democracy is complex but populism is simple.[34] In the nineteenth century, it took just four years for such simplification to take firm hold. "In

1892, before the depression brought popular discontents to a fever pitch," wrote Hofstadter, "General James B. Weaver campaigned on a well-rounded platform of reform issues." Not so those who followed him: "the growing demand for free silver so completely overshadowed other things in the minds of the people so as to fix them on a single issue that was at best superficial." The dreadful economic situation of the farmers of that time was caused by many factors: "tariffs, railroads, middlemen, speculators, warehousers, and monopolistic production of farm equipment." But the people could not be expected to follow the complexities of economics in the real world. And so in his 1896 campaign, Bryan offered them something that made intuitive sense: free silver would cause inflation that would lower the amount of their debt. "Bryan was content to stress free silver to the exclusion of everything else, and thus to freeze the popular cause at its lowest level of understanding," as Hofstadter put it. "It was the only time in the history of the Republic when a candidate ran for the presidency on the strength of a monomania."[35] At least until 2016.

Hofstadter could never let go of the theme of simplification. It dominated his book *Anti-Intellectualism in American Life*, for what made anti-intellectualism both possible and dangerous was its avoidance of anything complicated. In *The Paranoid Style in American Politics*, moreover, Hofstadter devoted considerable attention to William "Coin" Harvey, author of a wildly popular 1894 manifesto making the case for free silver. *Coin's Financial School* relates the fictional exploits of a young man who takes on the major financial figures of the day and bests them with commonsense arguments that appealed to the huge audience looking for answers to their financial plight. Complicated the book was not. "It had behind it," Hofstadter wrote, "the fierce logic of the one-idea mind, the firm conviction that complex social issues can be unraveled to the last point and pinned down for good, that social problems could be solved, and solved by simple means." With everything reduced to the problem of silver, "one is tempted to propound a Gresham's law of popular monetary discussion, by which the weak arguments drive the strong one out of circulation."[36] Free silver, for the populists, acted as a kind of displacement: it became a substitute for the real causes of popular frustration, displacing attention from where it belonged to a place where its complexities could be rendered with greater simplicity.

Others among the mature liberals elaborated on this theme. To Daniel Bell, figures such as Bryan, or, for that matter, McCarthy, were "terrible simplifiers," who flourish because we are an unsettled society in which, just as one could be more royalist than the king, "one becomes more traditionalist than even the settled families, and, in the case of nationality groups, more compulsively American than the older families." Populist movements, Bell believed, are a response to the anxieties of what Hofstadter had called "status politics," or the uncertainty generated by the fact that, in America, you can never be sure where you really stand in the social hierarchy. In this sense, the curse of populism is intimately connected to the blessings of social mobility.[37] It is because we lack firm status positions that status becomes so important in our politics.

Simplification certainly influenced the way the mature liberals understood the politics of the 1950s. "Today," Bell wrote, "the politics of the radical right is the politics of frustration—the sour impotence of those who find themselves unable to understand, let alone command, the complex mass society that is the polity today."[38] At a loss for what to do with respect to the hard issues of political economy and foreign policy, anti-communism gave the populistic right the appearance that it was tackling real-world problems. Listen to populists' own words, and they were dealing with the most important problem of all: what could be more serious than the existence of a top-secret conspiracy intent on ending the American way of life? But in reality, as David Riesman and Nathan Glazer argued, "charges of domestic Communism gave political leaders a way to seem active, strong, and rough without actually having a program."[39] McCarthy's efforts to appear a populist, in the view of the mature liberals, spoke to the recognition of American conservatives that without strenuous attempts at simplification—what today we would call single-issue politics—right-wing politicians would be in danger of losing their passionate following.

Over the course of time, simplification became even simpler. For Bryan, advocating free silver became an alternative to addressing the complexities of real social problems. With McCarthy, it was by no means clear that there was a real problem to be displaced. It is true that in the 1948 elections, the Communist Party seemed to be gaining respectability. But while Communist spies no doubt existed, communism simply was not the threat to democracy that it was in, say, Italy. Following Bryan would at least lead you back to the real issues of monopolization and price fixing. Follow the anti-Communist trail blazed by McCarthy all the way back, and you end up with pretty much nothing. Bryan's populism, in short, was a symbol of something else, while McCarthy's was just a symbol. The New Right of the 1950s, Riesman and Glazer wrote, was more about "atmosphere" than about any actual policies. "Its leaders cannot channel discontent; they can interpret it: they can explain why everything has gone wrong—for the while; that is enough. Thus, the picture today in American politics is of intelligence without force or enthusiasm facing force and enthusiasm without intelligence."[40] If populism leads away from the real world, symbolic populism avoids it completely. It would seem, then, that with respect to simplification, there is nowhere further to go: once the link between symbol and reality has been severed, politics will be little more than a campaign between illusions.

While simplification in the United States seemed to have gone as far as it could with McCarthyism, there was nonetheless one more step to take. A populist without a voice is a political loser; gaining exposure and winning converts, to the populist, are the same thing. This helps explain why populists, for all their nostalgia for a simpler way of life, tend to be quite familiar with, and to rely upon, any innovations in mass communications. Distrustful of the press, Bryan published his own newspaper, the *Commoner*, out of Lincoln, Nebraska. McCarthy and the press developed a two-way process beneficial to both: McCarthy would time his accusations to correspond with the press's publication schedule, while the press would give free publicity to the senator's charges, no matter how outlandish.[41] Activists such as Richard Viguerie, who developed the art of direct mail campaigns, fueled the growth of the contemporary American right along the same lines. It is also no coincidence that the one politician who can be viewed as a serious precursor of today's radical right, Senator Jesse Helms, got his start hosting a radio program.[42]

As much as Viguerie and Helms were innovators, however, they were still operating under the old rules of trying to win converts. In more recent years, an even more innovative approach to winning mass support originated with the men who helped elect Donald Trump: Rupert Murdoch and the late Roger Ailes. Their contribution was not to sever the link between a complicated reality and a simplified substitute but to break the link entirely by creating a new, and much easier to grasp, reality all to itself. A term used by opponents of their techniques, "epistemic closure," developed by a libertarian blogger named Julian Sanchez, characterizes it well.[43] The world of the contemporary populist follower is completely self-enclosed. Inside that world, Democrats are Socialists, President Obama is an illegal immigrant, Hillary Clinton is a felon, Donald Trump is a savior, and political correctness prevents any political leader save a conservative one from ever speaking the truth. Under epistemic closure, falsity is not measured by how far any statement deviates from reality but by whether the new reality it creates can sustain a mass audience. Also new in epistemic closure is not the method but the technology: one can use the speed of communication made possible by the Internet and social media to close out one world and live comfortably within another. Anything complicated, in this world, must, by definition, be false. There is only one reason why economic stagnation exists, our enemies gain victories, or bureaucracy is abused, and it always known to the populist leader and revealed, with great fanfare, to his or her followers in full block letters printed in bold, when not in a series of tweets.

The mature liberals wrote in a media environment totally different from our own. For them, false news could be countered, and while it might take a long time for the truth to emerge, emerge it generally did. This was the theme of an influential essay written during the Vietnam War by Hannah Arendt in response to the many lies of Lyndon Johnson. "Truth," she wrote, "though powerless and always defeated in a head-on clash with the powers that be, possesses a strength of its own." Truth has a ground to stand on, reality, while falsehood does not. Those who counter power with truth will therefore be rewarded "when reality takes its revenge on those who dare defy it."[44] Arendt was not known as an optimist—she wrote powerfully about "dark times"[45]—but her comments on truth and politics, in the context of today's media, seem naïve to a fault. When there are alleged to be many realities, and when all of them are given roughly equal credence, it is far more difficult for the real one to emerge and dispel the false ones.

The height of the era of epistemic closure may nonetheless be behind us. Fox News was discovered to have been the locus of considerable sexual harassment, the man most responsible for the creation of a new reality for the right, Roger Ailes, died before Trump had been a half year in office, and the Murdoch family could be in the process of changing its attitude toward the president. It could be the case, then, that we will retreat to ordinary anti-intellectualism. Perhaps this is actually good news. Compared to the populism of what appears in today's conservative media, ordinary anti-intellectualism would be a significant improvement: at least it allows a role for intellectuals.

Just as the mature liberals left socialism behind them, they also began to abandon the ideas of Karl Marx. But whom to put in his place? A former Trotskyite on the edges of their circle, James Burnham, had turned sharply to the right, and he recommended those he called "the Machiavellians": Vilfredo Pareto, Gaetano Mosca, and Roberto Michels.[46] The mature liberals did not go along; they wanted a thinker less tainted with fascism to express their disenchantment. Why not, then, Max Weber, the theorist for whom disenchantment expressed the key dilemma of modernity? Not only did Weber become a much-cited figure among the mature liberals, a piece in his huge corpus of writings became the core text. It was not Weber's enormously influential reflections on Protestantism and the rise of capitalism, nor his profound writings on bureaucracy. For the mature liberals, the

Weberian crucial text was a lecture he gave to students in Munich in 1919, published in English as "Politics as a Vocation." Its theme was the necessity of a politics of responsibility, a requirement if politics were to survive the modern demagogue. One ought to consider Weber's lecture as one of the great documents in the history of thinking about political maturity.

It is a shame that Weber never wrote about William Jennings Bryan. The idea is not as ludicrous as it sounds. The two men were contemporaries, and Weber had a surprisingly deep understanding of America. He had visited the St. Louis World's Fair in 1904, and had filled his writings with the thoughts of Benjamin Franklin and the trials and tribulations of the urban political boss. If Weber had written about Bryan's "Cross of Gold" speech, it is not difficult to imagine his theme. The rhetoric of that speech, especially when compared to the prescripted campaign speeches of today, is remarkably moving. But the romanticization of the common people and an argument based far more on emotion than reason would have made Weber shudder.

Weber drew a distinction between two kinds of politicians operating by two different sets of ethics. An ethic of "ultimate ends" is one in which a political leader pursues what he believes is the right path, and his conviction that he is on that path is so strong that consequences be damned. "If an action of good intent leads to bad results, then, in the actor's eyes, not he but the world, or the stupidity of other men, or God's will who made them thus, is responsible for the evil." The demagogue offers a clear example of this ethic. He can be found "where this striving for power ceases to be *objective* and becomes purely personal self-intoxication." As he becomes increasingly detached from the cause that brought him into the political ring, "his irresponsibility . . . suggests that he enjoy power merely for power's sake, without a substantive purpose." To say that Weber was critical of this kind of leader is an understatement. "There is no more harmful distortion of political force than the parvenu-like braggart with power and the vain self-reflection in the feeling of power, and in general every worship of power per se."[47] However much Weber's words sound like a warning about a future American president, his lecture anticipated something much closer to his home. Four years later, in the same city in which Weber had delivered his lecture, Adolf Hitler led the "Beer Hall Putsch," his political coming out. (Hitler became dictator a decade later by taking advantage of an emergency provision of the Weimar Constitution, written in 1919 with the help of Max Weber.)

In contrast to the ethic of ultimate ends was what Weber called an "ethic of responsibility." Anyone operating under this ethic understands that because power is also associated with violence, power must always be exercised cautiously. "Whoever contracts with violent means for whatever ends—and every politician does—is exposed to its specific consequences." This kind of leader, realizing that "politics is made with the head, not with other parts of the body or soul," keeps a certain distance from passionate political causes. One kind of distance is especially required: "The politician has to overcome a quite trivial and all-too-human enemy: a quite vulgar vanity, the deadly enemy of all matter-of-fact devotion to a cause, and of all distance, in this case, of distance towards one's self." Responsible politics cools down rather than heats up. In some of the most famous words ever written by a sociological theorist, Weber concluded that "not summer's bloom lies ahead of us, but rather a polar night of icy darkness and hardness, no matter which group may triumph now." The true vocation of politics lies with those willing to operate under such conditions by taking responsibility for their actions.[48]

Fortunately, Weber did have American disciples, and they took his themes to heart. Daniel Bell's thought resembled Weber's in many aspects, and he was fond of citing "Politics as a Vocation," which he believed offered a near-perfect expression of the great dilemma of the contemporary intellectual. Intellectuals want to fight destructive enemies with the best ideas available to them, but Weber's genius lay in resisting this heroic temptation, in warning them not to be smug-certain of the truths for which they fight. Bell admired those he called "prodigal sons"—those who, metaphorically speaking, leave home for radical movements only to come back wiser and more mature are to be admired. "A resilient society," Bell wrote, "like a wise parent, understands this ritual, and in meeting the challenge to tradition, grows."[49] Maturity, in such a way, would once again prove its value.

The ritual of returning home with greater wisdom marked many of the mature liberals; they were all, in their own ways, prodigal sons. Hofstadter, for example, quite familiar with the praise lavished on progressive historians such as Charles A. Beard when young, later rejected Beard's efforts to reduce history to economic motives.[50] Lionel Trilling wanted greater recognition of American literature but not at the cost of downplaying the greatness of English writers, such as Jane Austen and E. M. Forster. Nathan Glazer and Daniel Patrick Moynihan literally returned to the ethnic neighborhoods of their youth, but fortified with the tools of social science. And Niebuhr, the mature liberal with the greatest mastery of religious sources, never left the religion of his birth, but he also believed that "the whole story of modern culture might be truly chronicled in the parable of the Prodigal Son. The son who threw away his advantages may be a strong metaphor for the modern condition because at least he was autonomous, making his own decisions, however unwise."[51]

Like Max Weber, or, for that matter, William Jennings Bryan, Niebuhr thought long and hard about the relationship between religion and politics. Surprisingly, he came away somewhat sympathetic to the politics of Bryan. But not surprisingly at all, he also showed little sympathy for his religion. It bothered Niebuhr that the East Coast elite showed such contempt for the Great Commoner, whom he saw as "so fair a man" and "so innocent and pacific."[52] Evangelicalism, however, was another matter: it was much too strongly committed to what Niebuhr's former colleague Dietrich Bonhoeffer had called "cheap grace."[53] In his notes (published under the wonderful title *Leaves from the Notebook of a Tamed Cynic*), Niebuhr found evangelical Protestantism remarkably superficial: "Here we are living in a complex world in which thousands who have been 'won to Christ' haven't the slightest notion how to live a happy life or how to live together with other people without making each other miserable."[54] A religion that offers salvation with so few demands on those who would be saved cannot be taken seriously. Immaturity, it would seem, can characterize certain kinds of worship just as it can describe certain forms of politics.

From the perspective of the mature liberals, the single biggest sin tempting politicians is the irresponsibility that flows from a failure to treat politics with the seriousness it deserves. And that, as if to close the circle, is precisely what is wrong with populism: its view on politics remained infantile. It is difficult, for example, to think of one other political movement in American history that had such a close affinity with children's books: Ignatius Donnelly's books were frequently fantasies for children, and one of the great populist manifestos, written in 1900 by L. Frank Baum, a supporter of Bryan, was called *The Wonderful Wizard of Oz* and was filled with references to poor but honest farmers (the Scarecrow); oppressed urban workers (the Tin Man); and distant Washington, DC, the Emerald City. (The Wicked Witches of East and West, I believe, stand for, well, witches.) Just as populism is content with emphasizing one key theme, it always stays at one level of understanding. The mature liberals had, in the course of their lives, changed their positions, usually from socialism to liberalism or neoconservatism. Over the course of their lives, populists, too, changed their positions, all too often, as exemplified in the career of Georgia's Tom Watson, a fiery agrarian rebel who had been Bryan's running mate in 1896, only to become a racist and anti-Semite later in life.[55] But whatever they believed, they believed it with the innocence of a child. No prodigal sons could be found among them, for nothing much ever changed. Bryan, Hofstadter concluded, "closed his career in much the same role as he had begun it in 1896: a provincial politician following a provincial populace in provincial prejudices."[56]

As they contemplated the careers of political leaders who never rethought their first premises, the mature liberals could not help but be tempted by the language of psychology. Hofstadter was the most committed to this way of thinking, settling on the term "paranoia" to characterize people who, rather than adjust to a changing world, chose instead to believe in esoteric conspiracies. For this, he was severely criticized, especially by psychologists and psychiatrists. To me, the opposite of this charge makes more sense: Hofstadter and his fellow liberals were not psychological *enough*. In particular they failed to pay sufficient attention to a disorder much used in public discussion today: narcissism.

This is not true of a historian who both resembled Hofstadter and greatly admired him: Christopher Lasch, who did write, with enormous commercial success, about narcissism. But Lasch concentrated the bulk of his attention on the 1960s generation attracted to radical politics and alternative lifestyles; populists and Bryan are nowhere to be found in Lasch's *The Culture of Narcissism*.[57] Yet the fact that a raging narcissist such as Donald Trump could be taken seriously as a populist suggests that there is a disturbing codependent relationship between the populist hero and his or her audience. Populist leaders give sanction to their followers never to see anything unpleasant in the mirror he holds up to them. No follower of a populist is ever said to be wrong, misguided, prejudiced, or myopic. The populist audience is there to be flattered, pure and simple. If someone in the populist's audience loses control and submits to violence, his actions, however untoward, are always justifiable. Like the evangelicals flocking to megachurches, populist followers much prefer the soft sounds of believing themselves better people than harsh condemnation or admonitions to sober up. The elites, they believe, always manage to find their way of life suspect, calling it, among other things, racist, reactionary, or anti-intellectual. How refreshing for them to hear a politician telling them that their way of life is good and that he will not condemn them.

The narcissistic element in populism, I believe, explains two features of contemporary politics in America that have puzzled many observers. Because Ronald Reagan spoke in such sunny terms about America and its destiny, political observers came to the conclusion that voters will reject candidates who speak nothing but ill of their society. Yet populism nearly always speaks in harshly negative tones. Consider the 1892 Populist platform: "We meet in the midst of a nation brought to the verge of moral, political, and material ruin.

Corruption dominates the ballot-box, the Legislature, the Congress, and touches even the ermine of the bench. The people are demoralized. . . . The newspapers are largely subsidized or muzzled, public opinion silenced, business prostrated, homes covered with mortgages, labor impoverished, and the land concentrated in the hands of the capitalists."[58] The comparison to Donald Trump's rhetoric in 2016, with all its talk of America as a fear-driven and hopelessly corrupt society, is striking. What is it about such condemnatory rhetoric that so many Americans find sufficiently appealing? How can they like a man who seems to dislike them so?

The answer is that Americans interpreted Trump's speeches as rhetoric and judged them not on their content but on the sincerity of their delivery. Had the microphones been turned off when Trump spoke at the convention that nominated him for president, the audience, I wager, would still have cheered. Their minds were not going to be changed by anything Trump and his surrogates actually said. When their leaders condemned society as decadent and corrupt, they knew in their hearts that he was not condemning *them*. Between the leader and his following there lay a secret mutual understanding: however awful the world was, there was nonetheless a circle of the good, and they, fortunate to be born both American and white, were blessed enough to belong to it. In our day, populists talk to their followers in a kind of code that both understand but that the uninitiated find puzzling.

Trump's haste to drop much of his populist talk once president, focusing on a more traditional Republican platform of trying to end Obamacare, promote massive tax cuts for the rich, and support budget cuts that would cause serious pain to his own voters, should not have been a surprise. All populists cut back on their promises once they achieve office; if anything, Trump's decision to abandon populism once in office is a sign of just how much of a populist he is. Populism is a technique for gaining power, not exercising it. The populist's followers certainly do not care that much about the abandonment of the agenda endlessly repeated by their candidate; what they really crave is recognition of their grievances, and once that has been delivered, whether they get their fair share of tax cuts or federal expenditures or even whether health insurance is affordable, is not all that important. The idea that Trump was actually making promises that he expected to keep, and that his followers would be upset when he never followed through, does not accord with the realities of populist politics. It is futile and self-defeating, I believe, to take glee in pointing out how often Donald Trump violated his populistic campaign promises once in office. A good populist never meant those promises to be taken seriously. It is an inherent part of the politics of petulance that the psychology of Donald Trump resembles that of a child: demanding, selfish, impatient, and revengeful. If so, there is a reason for it: a political movement shaped by the authors of children's books not unnaturally can wind up with a leader who would find even those books difficult to read.

Populism is now so firmly fixed in America's political culture that even if a more mature leader were elected as Trump's successor, populism would doubtless come back. But I do think it will prove difficult to make itself felt again any time soon in Republican circles. In the wake of Trump's presidency, Republican politicians who lack whatever it is that makes Trump so appealing to his followers will likely be unable to pursue political programs that harm working-class Republican voters without paying an electoral price. The Republican Party's agenda has not altered much at all over the past two or three decades, and the simple truth is that its ideological parent, Ayn Rand, whatever else anyone may think of her, was anything but a populist. It takes a very special kind of demagogue to pursue policies so beneficial to the rich while not alienating the many more people who are not as well endowed. Perhaps Trump is that kind of demagogue or perhaps he will prove not to be. But whatever he does or does not do, one thing is certain: the Republican Party in the short run and maybe even in the long run will never deviate from its determination to reward the rich with even more riches. The Republican Party's success in passing a massive giveaway to the rich in its 2017 tax legislation was written in the party's DNA.

Populistic demagoguery proved so popular on the right during the 2016 election that many Democrats will surely want to adopt it for the left. It is inevitable, they believe, that Republicans will disappoint the angry white people that voted for them, and the best hope for the Democrats will be to win over those voters with policies that, they claim, will actually work to their benefit (even if their potential working-class allies do not seem to want them). "Populistic politics can play a crucial role in democratizing power and politics today," writes Laura Grattan, a political scientist.[59] For her, and many others, the appeal of being on the side of the people is just too great to resist. Populism gives leftists a path, or so they believe, to shed the Democrats' turn to the center that began with Bill Clinton and showed no sign of abating with his wife. Yet if Bernie Sanders or any other candidate runs in 2020 promising single-payer health insurance, which would require both mass public expenditures and the termination of work-related insurance plans that people currently have, once again populists will hold fast to the rule of never delivering on their promises.

Thus, populism is the dream that may never die. Populism, I believe, can be stopped only by what both Weber and the mature liberals called a politics of responsibility. There are not many politicians, in either party, who live by Weber's preferred ethic, and we are unlikely to find any so long as our campaigns and elections continue to be directed at five-year-olds. One can only hope that not too much time will pass before such a politician emerges.

One truth of the Trump years hopefully will never be lost. Populists are not supposed to win, for if they do, all their martyrdom is stripped away. (Only the improbability of winning can explain why the Trump campaign considered a Russian offer to provide "dirt" on Hillary Clinton. An unelected Trump would have been an unexamined Trump.) It therefore seemed to come as a surprise, even to Trump himself, as Michael Wolff's potboiler on the first nine months of the Trump presidency makes clear, that he won.[60] Democracy in America will be strengthened when populists do what they are supposed to do and become the stuff of legend. William Jennings Bryan, "the one American Poet who could sing outdoors," in the words of the poet Vachel Lindsay,[61] did exactly that. Outdoors is where Trump belongs, but, fascinated by and attracted to power as he is, it is where he will never voluntarily go.

3
THE RETURN OF MASS SOCIETY

Ever since Alexis de Tocqueville's eventful 1831 visit to the United States, where he arrived to examine prisons but found the whole of the American experience too fascinating to ignore, individuals from one country have sought to learn more about themselves by studying the people of another. As a new nation, America was the destination of a host of European visitors, from Frances Trollope, mother of the novelist, whose book *Domestic Manners of the Americans* was published in 1832, the same year as Tocqueville's *Democracy in America*, to the French philosopher Bernard-Henri Lévy, who repeated Tocqueville's trip in 2005.[1] For some, America was a refuge. For others, it was a sociological experiment.

The mature liberals generally confined themselves to the United States. But as scholars influenced by both Tocqueville and Max Weber, they also knew the importance of comparative social science. One task in particular struck them as essential to an understanding of American politics. If this country was so susceptible to populism and the demagoguery accompanying it, why not learn from comparing it to a country without such flaws? From this exercise, they drew a conclusion as important to them as their distrust of populism. What they concluded was, in fact, populism in reverse: should demagoguery get out of hand, democracy might require the firm guidance of elites to put itself back on the right track.

Those critics focused on a democratic society whose way of conducting politics seemed far more responsible—and by implication more responsive to the kinds of challenges raised by McCarthyism—than the American way: Great Britain. The sociologist Edward Shils was especially taken with England: "Great Britain," he wrote unambiguously, "has a better record in civil politics than any other country in the world."[2] The caustic critic Dwight Macdonald, who found so many faults with American mass culture, nonetheless admired English periodicals such as *The Spectator* as well as the BBC.[3] But the scholar who made the case for England in the context of McCarthyite demagoguery was Herbert Hyman, one of the pioneers of survey research. Ordinary Britons, Hyman speculated, were not all that different from ordinary Americans. Elites, however, were another matter entirely: "Insulated from popular pressures," British elites, as if characters in a play called *The Lonely Crowd*, were free "to follow their own inner directives."[4] Had Americans shown greater deference toward their leaders, he implied, their leaders would also have had greater flexibility in meeting the challenges posed by McCarthy. The trouble with our politics was not that our masses were uninformed, although that they were, but that they were insufficiently respectful. Just because these writers viewed Joe McCarthy as a danger to democracy, it did not follow that everything democratic was therefore good. Deference to the elites saved the English from anything like the Wisconsin demagogue. We suffer our fools, gladly or otherwise, because we do not trust our elites to control them.

For better or worse, this comparison has not stood the test of time. The British proved in their 2016 Brexit vote that they were quite capable of showing little or no deference to the wishes of their political elites. Demagogic leaders such as Boris Johnson, the former mayor of London, and Nigel Farage, the leader of the UK Independence Party, which led the campaign against the European Union, seemed to shape their strategy as if they had carefully studied American populism. It worked: many Britons did not know what they were voting for and were quite surprised to learn afterward that their votes actually carried consequences. Brexit, furthermore, was a referendum, a device associated with methods of direct democracy such as the recall and the initiative, which were justified by the argument, so American in nature, that the wisdom of middle-class common sense can be relied upon to return power to the people. It is difficult to think of any decision in the world today that was both more democratic and more dangerous than the vote for Brexit. Not even Donald Trump's decision to withdraw from the Paris climate change agreement comes close, for his actions did not have the *direct* endorsement of the people, while the actions of the Brexit leaders did. The differences between the two countries disappeared, in short, not because America matured more toward the British model, but because British democracy deteriorated in an American direction.

We are now living through a period of democratic unhappiness everywhere, which is both simplifying and complicating the task of insuring democracy's future. Two forces are clashing with each other, with no resolution in sight. One is democracy, which in the years since the mature liberals wrote, has continued its advance. This may sound like a strange thing to say in the United States at a time when state legislators, nearly all of them Republican, are trying their best to limit suffrage in ways that will benefit their party. Nor does it help that the Supreme Court in *Citizens United* allowed huge amounts of money to flow into campaigns, thereby rewarding those who have the money to spend. In many ways, however, these actions were taken precisely because the country was becoming more democratic. Although Congress has been paralyzed, no longer can single members from one-party districts hold up legislation, as was the case with anti–civil rights southern politicians a half century ago. Candidates for president, in addition, are no longer chosen by brokers and bosses, as they were in the 1950s, but, for the most part, by primary voters in the states. (Hold whatever views you want about Donald Trump and Hillary Clinton, but majorities of those who voted within their parties selected both.) Televised debates, which did not exist when the mature liberals wrote, may not satisfy policy wonks, but they do enable candidates to differentiate themselves from one another. On top of all this, new social media have enabled politicians to communicate directly with their followers, bypassing mediating institutions: government by Twitter is what you get when elites evaporate. The only fly in our largely democratic ointment, though it is a large one, is that a victory in the Electoral College can override a popular vote majority, but even that wound up favoring the more populistic candidate in 2016.

This increasingly democratic political culture, however, has only added to already high levels of public discontent in democracies all around the globe: both the United States and the United Kingdom have, in recent years, been governed by leaders with exceptionally negative approval ratings. Party systems are giving people what they choose but not necessarily what they want. We thus live in a political cycle in which citizens respond to the messages of outsiders, hoping that they will bring some fresh air, only to turn on them when they disappoint, thereby starting the cycle over. The distrust of politics and suspicion toward government are as high as they have ever been. It is a striking development when greater democracy simply causes unhappier democracy.

As if this were not a serious enough problem, the expansion of democracy has come about in an era when liberal democratic societies find themselves at the most momentous crossroads they have faced since their decision to go to war against Nazi Germany. I am referring to the rise of populistic nationalism. Democratic societies can try to alleviate the anger so many of their citizens feel by turning inward and responding to nationalist sentiments, but then they cut themselves off from the international economic and political arrangements that have enabled the West to survive in peace since the end of the Second World War. Or they can decide, as difficult as it may be, that this is precisely the time to strengthen once again global alliances and international commitments to deal with challenges, such as global warming, that no nation can address by itself. The old divisions of left and right are not very helpful at this time. But the choice between elite and mass is. If the people themselves are given the option of choosing, they will likely respond in a nationalist fashion. If the elites make the decision, they are likely to join together with elites in other countries at the expense of what their own citizens would rather do.

Expressed this way, only one possible answer seems likely to preserve democratic arrangements, and that is to do what the people want: if Trump is the duly elected choice of the American people, then let him find the political room to act as president without constant attack, and if the British people really wish to leave the European Union, then the sooner, the better. Here, I believe, is where the wisdom of the mature liberals is most necessary. For it is in fact the other path—the one that questions whether more democracy is the solution to democratic unease—that is far more likely, as paradoxical as it may sound, to help democracy survive. During this period of what Edward Luce has called "the retreat of Western liberalism," democracy may be its own worst enemy.[5]

I here make the case not so much that we have too much democracy, but that we have too much of the wrong kind. First, I will discuss a concept that was important to the mature liberals, even if it has been in abeyance since: mass society. Then I will examine some recent empirical research into America's version of nationalistic populism to judge whether or not the concept of mass society remains relevant. Finally, I will attempt to show why, in paying so much attention to *who* votes, Western societies, and especially the United States, are paying insufficient attention to *why* they vote in the first place.

As time goes by, Hannah Arendt's accomplishments in *The Origins of Totalitarianism* only grow greater. She published her book in a language not her mother tongue. It was finished in 1950, only five years after the Allies had brought the war against Nazism to a close. The book was far longer than most nonfiction books, and it contained numerous references to prominent German philosophers such as Hegel and Nietzsche. Yet it was widely translated, won numerous literary prizes, and was enthusiastically praised by reviewers. Her friend Mary McCarthy wrote her to say that it was "a truly extraordinary piece of work, an advance in human thought of, at the very least, a decade, and also engrossing and fascinating in the way a novel is."[6] Most remarkable of all, when Donald Trump was elected in 2016, Arendt's book, more than sixty years old, shot to the higher reaches of the Amazon.com best-seller list.

At the heart of Arendt's analysis lay the concept of mass society. "The totalitarian movements," she wrote, "aim at and succeed in organizing masses—not classes, like the old interest parties of the Continental nation-states; not citizens with opinions about, and interests in, the handling of public affairs, like the parties of the Anglo-Saxon countries."[7] Classes fashion a kind of political geography in which class location generally determines voting preferences; at least in two-party systems, one party tends to represent the well-off and the other the not-so-well-off. Citizens, moreover, are individuals who on the one hand have the right to vote and on the other hand accept that voting imposes certain obligations, such as gaining at least minimal political knowledge or taking their responsibilities seriously before casting a ballot and routinely exercising the franchise. It is because of these rights and obligations that Arendt wrote so powerfully about statelessness: "Man is a social animal," she wrote in "We, Refugees," "and life is not easy for him when social ties are cut off."[8] Depriving people of political status as statelessness does is like cutting off one of their arms; since having a political identity is so large a part of what makes us human, statelessness is a precondition for destroying everything human about us. Citizenship, and with it the right to vote, are gifts of the highest value.

A society in which the masses flourish is utterly different. Its members are isolated and alienated. They act politically out of fear and rarely react rationally. Solidarity for them is a negative reaction, not a positive emotion. Public unhappiness, Arendt wrote in *The Origins of Totalitarianism*, had produced "one great unorganized, structureless mass of furious individuals who had nothing in common except their vague apprehension that the hopes of party members were doomed, that, consequently, the most respected, articulate and representative members of the community were fools and that all the powers that be were not so much evil as they were equally stupid and fraudulent."[9] Those who live in a mass society do vote, but uninformed and emotional votes only reinforce, rather than weaken, the irrationality upon which mass society is built. The theory of mass society, with its startling images of mass man destroying everything in its path, offered a rich home for pessimists, none more prominent than the Spanish philosopher José Ortega y Gasset.[10] No one who believed that progress was always present and always, or at least most of the time, positive could reside in it. Mass society is a place where the great gift of citizenship is returned unopened.

Arendt took great pains to elaborate one especially key difference between a society divided by classes and one under the influence of the masses. Classes have interests: their members involve themselves in politics in order to increase the share of the benefits they receive from public authorities, especially government. Liberalism developed as a theory dealing with the clash between interests: so long as conflicting groups express their demands in visible and resolvable ways, the state can act as a peaceful adjudicator between them; this was, simply put, the guiding idea of the framer of the American Constitution James Madison. To be sure, the wealthy classes will win most such contests, which is why liberalism became the favorite political philosophy of the rising bourgeoisie. But liberalism also left at least some room for the unfavored classes to obtain something, perhaps a welfare state or, in the case of Northern European democracies, an emerging Social Democratic state. Liberalism keeps the peace by giving some here and some there, always hoping to find a sustainable balance between those making conflicting demands on the state. In an odd way, the liberal state is apolitical. Ask it to increase the take-home pay of workers or to lessen the tax burden on their bosses, and it can respond. Ask it to give meaning and a sense of purpose to those who live within its borders, and it is generally at a loss.

Totalitarian movements and states respond to the empty moral hole the liberal state leaves behind by requiring what Arendt called a "demand for total, unrestricted, and unconditional loyalty of the individual," not to the party so much as to the leader. Totalitarian rulers know nothing of interests but do understand feelings: for them, the fracturing of society into interests stands in the way of the unanimity a totalitarian state needs to express the essential soul of a people. For such a task, individual initiative is not only frowned upon but made impossible. "Total domination does not allow for free initiative in any field of life, for any activity that is not entirely predictable. Totalitarianism in power invariably replaces all first-rate talents, regardless of their sympathies, with those crackpots and fools whose lack of intelligence and creativity is still the best guarantee of their loyalty."[11] Totalitarianism, in short, offers those who live in mass society a deal: give up your individuality, and we will provide the meaning of life you are missing. We are so sure that this will work that, if you resist, we will force it upon you.

With respect to mass society, there was, however, one hope: Arendt was not convinced that the idea applied to her new home. "America, the classical land of equality of condition and of general education with all its shortcomings," she wrote, "knows less of the modern psychology of the masses than perhaps any other country in the world."[12] Whether or not she was correct in this form of American exceptionalism, it became one of the major subjects of the mature liberals.

Most of the mature liberals agreed with Arendt that the European fear of mass society need not overly preoccupy them. Daniel Bell said of the theory of mass society: "Marxism apart, it is probably the most influential social theory in the Western world today."[13] But Bell found it flawed with respect to America, because it did not account for the rapid innovations in which the country specialized; in a sense, Bell voted for Tocqueville over Arendt. Although Tocqueville's concerns about the tyranny of the majority seemed to anticipate the theory of mass society, his argument that Americans were a nation of joiners suggested that they were not especially susceptible to emotional appeals based on loneliness and longing. As Seymour Martin Lipset put it, relying on empirical data, people "who belong to associations are more likely than others to give the democratic answer to questions concerning tolerance and party systems, to vote, or to participate actively in politics."[14]

After Bell, the theory of mass society never quite took hold in academia, though it did produce one significant book—*The Politics of Mass Society* (1959) by the sociologist William Kornhauser, all but forgotten now, but a major step in making the theory a serious topic for research. Kornhauser attempted to reconcile two general approaches to mass society, one associated with the aristocratic critique of democracy and the other with the democratic critique of liberalism, and he emphasized that "weak intermediate relations leave elites and non-elites exposed to one another, and thereby invite widespread mass behavior."[15] Mass society theory also influenced the work of C. Wright Mills and those dealing with the mass media. The theory's disposition in favor of elites, finally, struck a chord among cultural critics, such as the British philosopher Roger Scruton on the right and second-generation followers of the Frankfurt school on the left.

But the real problem with the theory, at least in the academic world, was not that it was foreign but that it was popular. Books such as William H. Whyte's *The Organization Man*, *The Status Seekers* and *The Hidden Persuaders* by Vance Packard, Erich Fromm's *Escape from Freedom*, *The Man in the Gray Flannel Suit* by Sloan Wilson, and Betty Friedan's *The Feminine Mystique* filled the shelves with speculations about conformity, alienation, and bureaucracy, leaving little left over for social theorists to ponder. Americans did not need social scientists to teach them about the theory of mass society because best-selling authors did that for them. "Why read the sociologists," Dwight Macdonald asked, "when Mr. Packard gives you their gist painlessly?"[16]

Macdonald, an intellectual but not an academic, was in a good position to override the objections of the professors and draw out the implications of where mass society might lead us. "A mass society," as he put it, "like a crowd, is inchoate and uncreative. Its atoms cohere not according to individual liking or traditions or even interests but in a purely mechanical way, as iron filings of different shapes and sizes are pulled toward a magnet working on the one quality people have in common." The problem of mass society, Macdonald insisted, lay not just with the masses: cheapness and vulgarity were increasingly influencing the cultural choices of the better-educated middle and upper-middle classes as well. Masscult, as Macdonald called the lowest form of human cultural achievement, "attempts to provide distraction to the tired businessman—or the tired proletarian. This kind of art is necessarily at a distance from the individual since it is specifically designed to affect not only what differentiates him from everybody else—that is what is of liveliest interest to him—but rather to work on the reflexes he shares with everybody else."[17] The American middle classes, however, especially in the years after World War II, were becoming increasingly sophisticated, and as they did, they demanded something that would show themselves to be superior intellectually to the mass audience watching insipid television, yet at the same time untaxed by anything as demanding as a Henry James novel, a Wordsworth poem, or a Bartok string quartet. Thus was born Macdonald's famous concept of Midcult, something artistically superior to what the masses were consuming but still falling far short of great works of art or literature. Think Book of the Month Club, the Revised Standard Version of the Bible, or Rodgers and Hammerstein.

Macdonald's proclivities, there can be no doubt, were unabashedly elitist. "Let the majority eavesdrop," he wrote," but their tastes should be firmly ignored." He, like many of his peers, was attracted by Matthew Arnold's ideal of teaching "the best that has ever been thought and written."[18] So elitist were Macdonald's views that, unlike other mature liberals, he doubted that anything much could be done to stop the proliferation of either Masscult or Midcult or that reform of either cult was possible. "Those who advocate this," he wrote, "start off with the assumption that there has already been a great advance in the diffusion of culture in the last two centuries—Edward Shils is sure of this, Daniel Bell thinks it is probably the case—and that the main problem is how to carry this further." Macdonald was far more pessimistic. Worrying him was "a narcotized acceptance of Masscult-Midcult and of the commodities it sells as a substitute for the unsettling and unpredictable (hence unsalable) joy, tragedy, wit, change, originality and beauty of real life." Midcult and Masscult share this: they tend toward happy endings. The more sober mature liberals would consider people like him, Macdonald wrote, "as either disgruntled Left romantics or reactionary dreamers or both." He did not object to either label: romance and reaction were, in his view, both preferable to uninspiring mass taste.[19]

The cultural criticism of the mature liberals is still read and even discussed today; Macdonald's writings are still in print, attracting readers who love sharp (and funny) prose. Yet in our far more democratic times, those writing in defense of great works of cultural achievement are generally viewed as arrogantly out of touch and as unsympathetic to a contemporary perspective focused on race, gender, or some other status. The paradoxical mix that the mature liberals tried to preserve—high culture and left-wing politics—was not very stable to begin with, and both public and academic attention largely turned away from highbrow writers.

We have, I believe, lost something important in our politics by not heeding what writers such as Macdonald were trying to teach us about mass society. A brief application of his ideas about culture to the realm of politics may help us here. When populism first emerged in the 1890s, it was firmly Masscult avant la lettre: Bryan spoke to the common man, and while his rhetoric was flowery, he never spoke over the heads of his followers. Bryan was to politics as Norman Rockwell later was to art: capable enough in technique, but incapable of anything that challenges the imagination.

If populism was Masscult, Progressivism, with its strong mainline Protestant outlook on the world, was Midcult. Politicians from superior social classes, such as the Roosevelts, spoke of reform in decidedly upper-class tones. As leaders in a democracy, they could never reach Shakespearean heights, but at least they appealed to higher sentiments than the base emotions populists preferred. The difference between Masscult and Midcult was evident in the 1950s in the contrast between Dwight D. Eisenhower and Adlai Stevenson, one of whom the people trusted and the other of whom the intellectuals respected. Midcult may have peaked in America's politics during the three years in which John F. Kennedy was president: Robert Frost recited one of his poems, "The Gift Outright," at Kennedy's inauguration, and Pablo Casals, the Yo-Yo Ma of the 1960s, played his cello in the Kennedy White House. In Macdonald's view, Frost was a "fine poet," but he found it telling that Frost had to clown around—he was a "natural showman"[20]—as if putting words down on paper was not sufficient to secure his reputation as an artist of the first rank. The Kennedys had their vicious side, but they were not to be accused, at least so long as Jacqueline Kennedy was in the White House, of catering to mass tastes. The presidents who succeeded Kennedy could.

In the years since JFK, one can imagine Macdonald saying, American politics has taken steps backward from Midcult to Masscult. It is all there on the public stage: Lyndon Johnson's toilet, Nixon's insecurities, the B-movie career of Ronald Reagan and his wife's need for an astrologer, the mama's boy charm of Bill Clinton, and the limited vocabulary and even more limited imagination of Donald Trump. American politics has returned to the Age of Bryan; speaking as if to a fifth grader has become the rule for all politicians, conservative as well as liberal. Such is what a democracy under the guidance of mass society becomes. No wonder it fails to inspire: it is not designed to do so. American politics, like a TV sitcom, is just too unsufferingly scripted to be worth the attention of mature people.

For anyone who believes that we have arrived at a crucial crossroads in our history, this is likely the worst time to suffer populism's fools. The decisions that American leaders will be making over the next decade or two will reverberate through issues as diverse as global warming, North Korea's development of nuclear weapons, rates of opioid-inducing addiction that threaten the future of America's poor, an ever-widening income gap that becomes more entrenched year by year, successful infiltration of our elections by the Russians, intensifying religious conflict, homegrown terrorism, an increasingly divisive Supreme Court, and even a possible stock market crash. If one is satisfied that Donald Trump is just the right kind of president to handle these matters, and even if one believes that the ever-cautious Hillary Clinton would have been, the mature liberals have nothing to offer. But if one thinks our democracy ought to be working better than this, at the least offering us candidates we can admire, there may be wisdom in the concerns of mature liberals about a society increasingly governed by the masses.

There is a good reason for the spike in interest in Arendt's *The Origins of Totalitarianism* following the election of Donald Trump: its passages about fury and disenchantment seem to describe what took place among the mass electorate in 2016, and Arendt's reflections on statelessness could not be more relevant than at a time when the United States has (once again) begun to close its borders. True, Arendt was a philosopher, not a sociologist; her reflections are not tied to all that many concrete empirical examples. Today, however, we have many social scientists and historians interested in how right-wing populist voters think and act. Their work can help us explore whether populist voters' political attitudes have come to embody the fears expressed by adherents of the theory of mass society.

Perhaps the most relevant such study is sociologist Arlie Russell Hochschild's *Strangers in Their Own Land*.[21] Persuaded that the political divide in America had created walls that needed to be breached, Hochschild moved to rural Louisiana, near Lake Charles, to try to discover its residents' feelings about America and its direction. These people closely resemble the southern plain folk to whom William Jennings Bryan addressed his remarks during the Scopes trial (although they are more likely to be Roman Catholic than evangelical Protestant). They are also, as Hochschild points out, among those who would benefit from an active government. Yet many if not most of them had been attracted to the Tea Party and would constitute the basis of Trump's eventual victory in the state. After attending one of Trump's rallies, Hochschild concluded that Donald Trump was like the revivalist preachers who once trod the same ground, offering hope and even possible redemption. The importance of Trump lay not so much in what he said but in how he made vulnerable people, or, needless to say, white people, feel that they mattered once again.

Another account of the ordinary Americans who find the politics of today's radical right attractive is provided in the work of historian Bethany Moreton.[22] The people about whom she writes live not far from Hochschild's subjects: in the Ozark region, where Arkansas, Oklahoma, Missouri, and a slight touch of Kansas meet. The most significant export of that region is the Walmart chain of superstores. One of the largest companies in the world, Walmart is known for its intense anti-union policies, its frequent commingling of business practice with one form or another of evangelical religion, its reliance on part-time workers, its low prices helped along by its low pay, its friendly relations with the world of country music, and its discriminatory policies in hiring and promoting. Despite its overarching paternalism, and that its products are relentlessly Masscult, its workers in general like the company and are proud to tell others how much. Although Moreton wrote before the Trump phenomenon emerged, she describes in vivid detail the world of the individuals who would come to vote for him.

This pattern of support for policies that seem to harm the people who support them is hardly a characteristic of southern folkways alone. Political scientist Katherine J. Cramer undertook a similar investigation in the state of Wisconsin.[23] She too conducted her research before Trump, but she did not need him: her state was already at the epicenter of a plan launched by right-wing industrialists Charles and David Koch with the help of the governor, Scott Walker, who has spent much of his time in office attacking unions, cutting the budget, and launching campaigns against the faculty in the state's once impressive university system. The wall that Cramer explores is the one between rural and urban individuals, and what most stands out is the former's almost uniform hatred of what they see as a distant and unfeeling government. With Hochschild and Moreton, one can say, intensity rather than direction has changed over the years, as very conservative states became extremely conservative states. Wisconsin is different. It was not only one of the most progressive of all the American states, McCarthy excepted; it was also among the most enlightened, proving to its citizens the value of expert advice and civic education.

As a result, in part, of the influence of books such as Cramer's, Moreton's, and Hochschild's, along with others such as the memoir of the Appalachia-born but Yale-trained lawyer J. D. Vance, a set of assumptions about why the right had become so powerful began to emerge in popular discourse.[24] The key to Donald Trump's victory, the story ran, was that Trump was a political outsider, not responsible for, and therefore not corrupted by, Washington and its distant ways, thereby enabling him, despite his enormous personal wealth, to run as a populist. It is true, this type of account continued, that Trump did not know much about the world, but this did not disturb his supporters, some of whom were what political scientists call "low-information voters" and others of whom were convinced that all politicians lie all the time. In spite of this cynicism, however, Trump's supporters did not necessarily believe that *he* was lying; in fact, they thought he was the only truth-teller at a time when everyone else seemed self-censored by considerations of political correctness. Liberals despised him; all the more reason, then, for these voters to despise liberals. True, there may have been significant elements of racism in Trump's makeup; indeed, there is little question but that white Americans were making race a major element of their electoral choices in the years leading up to Trump's victory. But to reduce the whole story of his support to that one propensity fails to account for what made him so different from other demagogues, such as George Wallace. Finally, it was becoming obvious to these voters that the United States, once the most religious of all the world's liberal democracies, was becoming less so, leading those who retained a strong sense of faith, especially evangelical Christians, to vote for a thrice-married man with no discernible spirituality who nonetheless endorsed their sense of looming national decay. We need, the conclusion ran, a new way of thinking to account for the success of right-wing populists in recruiting Middle Americans to their worldview. "Rather than an individualism that asserted autonomy and independence," Moreton summarized, "their version resonated with the language of self-esteem, the 'craving for significance' in a mass society that vernacular Christian theologians popularized in these same years: not 'Who am I?' but 'Whose am I?'"[25] Liberals may not agree with the right-wing views of these people, the argument ran, but they ought at least to acknowledge what moved them. If they do not, liberals are unlikely ever to win back all those white voters in the heartland of the country that had left the Democratic Party, Clinton's and Obama's party, behind.

One question in particular is settled by these accounts. In all three of these treatments, low-information voting was not the major problem. It is likely the case—no evidence is reported either way—

that these individuals could not name their state's senators or their congressman. Nonetheless, these people knew a great deal about the immediate world around them. The major force shaping the lives of those with whom Hochschild spoke, for example, including how long they themselves would lead them, is the pervasive pollution by petrochemical firms. Yet even though they have powerful childhood memories of hunting and fishing, and even knowing that they no longer do because of the new levels of pollution, they still tend to be pro-business. While some attributed the cases of cancer around them to unlucky genes, most knew where the real cause lay. They were also cognizant that there is something called the Environmental Protection Agency that is supposed to regulate the activities of polluting companies, but they do not trust it. Some of them had read in the newspapers about climate change, even if they did not believe everything they read. They could never be accused of ignorance: "Everyone I talked to," Hochschild commented, "was enduring a great deal of pollution and despite the silence from companies, politicians, and state officials, nearly everyone clearly knew it."[26]

Over in the Ozarks, a similar situation existed. If the Ozarks are now known for Walmart, its two major exports just a few decades ago, aside from country-and-western music, were evangelicalism and populism. Both, and especially the latter, have helped shape Walmart's corporate culture. "The economic vision of some Populist leaders," Moreton reminds us, "included large-scale buying cooperatives and producers' monopolies over the marketing of whole farm sectors. The federal intervention they sought in transportation, finance, and agriculture, which sounds so out of character for Wal-Mart Country today, was intended to help them join the monopolies rather than beat them." Homespun populism found itself adjusting with no significant tensions to family-and-faith-centered capitalism, as if Walmart's strategic plans for growth were developed with the assistance of both William Jennings Bryan and Norman Vincent Peale. It surely counts as one of the great ironies of American history that a movement designed to help the fortunes of America's farmers and low-wage workers wound up providing the tone, passion, and religiosity of the most reactionary of corporate bosses. "The legacy of Populism, the social capital of a female labor force, and the Christian tradition of sacred service," Moreton concluded, "all contributed to a distinct corporate model, a specific work process, and a new definition of skill and power."[27] One reason why so many people in the Ozarks never dream of protesting Walmart's wages or its discriminatory hiring policies is because Walmart's culture is their culture. They are content there because it feels like home.

Nor do the Wisconsinites with whom Cramer spoke appear to be ignorant of the issues that bother them. Starting with a question to rural residents about what irked them, she obtained responses such as this: "One thing we were bitching about yesterday is that you—is the state's penchant for unfunded mandates—what three times two times they got a referenda in the community that was not wanted. And so now—they keep jamming the cost down to the county so they can avoid spending it on the state's nickel, that has to stop."[28] The discussion then moved to the subject of whether state funding for the schools is equitable before concluding with their feeling that the cities were receiving the bulk of all the funds spent on higher education. One assumes that these individuals would not be familiar with academic work on distributive justice, but, as Cramer notes, that is what they were discussing. Information was plentiful, in short, and a surprising amount of it had reached those who would be affected by public policies.

From the standpoint of insuring democracy's future health, the fact that these people were *not* low-information voters would seem to be good news. Actually, the opposite is true. While we might wish that the rise of demagogues could be explained by voters who do not know what such politicians are doing and simply need better education, the real danger to democracy, as I will argue in the concluding chapter, lies in people who know exactly what demagogues are doing and support them anyway. This was an issue Arendt addressed in *The Origins of Totalitarianism*: why were totalitarian leaders such as Hitler and Stalin popular? It cannot, Arendt wrote, "be attributed to the victory of masterful and lying propaganda over ignorance and stupidity. . . .

For the propaganda of totalitarian movements . . . is invariably as frank as it is mendacious."[29] Thus if we take the theory of mass society seriously, these people do not have ignorance as an excuse. They may be voting for politicians who show little or no compassion toward poor people and minorities because they really believe that the plight of poor people and minorities imposes no obligation on themselves—even if they are poor. If racism, moreover, lies at the bottom of their preferences, perhaps their racism is explained by the fact that that they genuinely do not care for people of color. (Katherine Cramer did not find all that much explicit racism among rural Wisconsinites.) It means one thing if people want their politicians to vote against a national system of health insurance, but it means something far more uncomfortable if they are willing to suffer from a personal lack of insurance in order to support an ideology that would make others, whom they deem insufficiently deserving, suffer even more. Unthinking political reaction may be bad, but thoughtful political reaction is worse. There is something frightful in the way so many people react to those even less fortunate than they are. Are you so angry, one wants to ask them, that, despite your self-professed religiosity, you have simply run out of compassion?

A second issue raised by these writers, especially by Hochschild, is whether the views of the Trump supporters tell us something about them that is not necessarily visible on the surface. Hochschild found the reason for the conservatism of her respondents in what she calls "the deep story." "A deep story," she explained, "is a *feels-as-if-story*—it's the story feelings tell, in the language of symbols. It removes judgment. It removes fact. It tells us how things feel. Such a story permits those on both sides of the political spectrum to stand back and explore the *subjective prism* through which the party on the other side sees the world. And I don't believe we understand anyone's politics, right or left, without it." Under the influence of their deep story, the people with whom she spoke viewed themselves as patient and fair-minded, politely waiting in line until their turn would come. Yet other people, they insist, people different from them in race and religion, have been cutting in line ahead of them. For them, then, the enemy was not the corporations; it was "the local welfare office and the mailbox where undeserved disability and SNAP stamps arrive."[30] (SNAP is the current name for food stamp programs.) Instead of being punished, the rule-breakers were being rewarded while they themselves, in their view the good people, were losing out. They were attracted to Trump because, by one means or another, he would get those line-jumpers out of the way.

A democratic society should unquestionably respect the deepest stories that belong to its citizens, for it is here, in our inner conscience, where we develop aids to help us account for the world, that true individualism lives. The problem, though, is that when Hochschild begins to tell her readers about the deep stories of these people she presents them as a singular deep story, without generally attributing its particulars to distinct individuals. A collective deep story is totally different from a private one. Nearly all of Hochschild's respondents tell the same story, and it nearly always insists that government is ignoring their needs. And it's not just there that this story is told: on this point, Cramer's subjects in Wisconsin seem indistinguishable from Hochschild's in Louisiana, for, as Cramer put it, the Wisconsinites' animosity toward government "is partly about feeling overlooked, ignored, and disrespected." When so many stories are all the same, we are likely not dealing with the inner light of deep Protestant traditions but the rumor and gossip of Fox News. One of Cramer's respondents sounds as if she had just been watching Bill O'Reilly and Sean Hannity: "I really feel like there is too much free shit in the world that people are abusing. Way too much."[31] Collectively these "deep stories" sound, in fact, remarkably shallow: they reflect the kind of excuses that people have learned to use to cloak their lack of compassion. I would call this kvetching, the politics of petulance rendered into Yiddish, rather than deep storytelling. It is something of a stretch in contemporary America to feel overlooked when your political party holds all the levers of government. Think how we academics must feel.

Hochschild makes an impassioned case for respecting people's feelings. Yet her account of why so many people are attracted to the right, while no doubt accurate, is also not very reassuring, for, when it comes to mass society, feelings count far more than facts. The way people in Louisiana talk about facts and feelings leaves the impression that, unlike citizens in a liberal political world, they have no interests at all, no actual programs or policies that would respond to their needs and balance them against the needs of others. Attending that Trump rally, Hochschild observed that "his supporters have been in mourning for a lost way of life. Many have become discouraged, others depressed. They yearn to feel pride but instead have felt shame."[32] There is little doubt that the people attracted to Trump feel pain. The question left unanswered is whether the election of him, or any other candidate, can relieve it. Relief of pain, alas, is the province of physicians, not politicians. If we ask our candidates to lift the depression people feel, they are only likely to become even more depressed.

Feelings, moreover, are, in the term used by the philosopher Richard Rorty, "conversation stoppers."[33] Bob Hardy, one of Hochschild's respondents, was angry. "I've had enough of *poor me*," he told her. "I don't like the government paying unwed mothers to have a lot of kids, and I don't go for affirmative action. I met this one black guy who complained he couldn't get a job. Come to find out he's been to *private* school. I went to a local public school like everyone else I know."[34] Hardy does not believe that he is a racist. (Racists rarely do.) It really does not matter whether or not he was, at least for my purposes here. What does matter is that when feelings enter the picture, compromise and negotiation, both central to democracy, leave. Try to reason with Mr. Hardy. Ask him if he knows that Louisiana ranks fourth in the country in terms of benefits received from the federal government in relation to taxes paid in.[35] Or you can ask him if the black mother raising three kids while holding down two or three low-wage jobs so that her children can enjoy a middle-class lifestyle deserves a bit more respect. Mr. Hardy's comments were made in the context of a discussion of affirmative action, and no issue in American politics, I venture, is as vulnerable to subjective anecdotes as that one. Feelings are for one's family and friends. Protecting the democracy we all share requires a far greater respect for facts.

Finally, there is reason to doubt that Trump supporters feel a threat from the secular culture around them and are reacting against that. True, nearly all of them appear to be deeply religious. Jack Gray, a labor organizer in the Ozarks, described his frustrations with Walmart workers this way: "They are just one hundred percent about their churches, don't think the union means anything to them, and they won't say anything bad about the employers." But if love of God is an explanation for politically conservative beliefs, we ought to be clear about the kind of God these people worship. One of the area's leading religious leaders, Pastor H. D. McCarty, who identifies himself in a YouTube video as the "Razorback rabbi,"[36] told Moreton that in the recent past "we were one the fastest-growing churches in America." His church grew because doctrine took second place to meeting people's needs. "We begin from the premise," McCarty continued, "that Jesus is at the center of everything, so there is no sacred versus profane—it's all sacred."[37] This, however, is megachurch talk, not that of the old time religion of William Jennings Bryan. McCarty now heads Ventures for Christ Inc. at Ecclesia College in Fayetteville, Arkansas. Like so many contemporary evangelical leaders, he measures his success by the number of converts, not by the depth of their commitment. When such an individual says that the whole word is sacred, he is really acknowledging the importance of the techniques he uses to reach his expanding flock, such as television ministry, small group meetings, blogs, Facebook, twelve-step recovery, and what he calls "graphic theology," or the use of illustrated materials—let's call them comic books—to teach the proper approach to Jesus.[38] That may be why so many evangelicals voted for Trump. Their desire to express hostility toward immigrants and people of color is stronger than any desire to speak about compassion, oneness with the world, and the sacred. Religious they are. Otherworldly they are not.

An application of Arendt's ideas about mass society might offer a better explanation of the political attitudes and behavior of these Americans than low information, deep stories, feelings, or faith-based reasoning. No longer protected by strong labor unions, disgusted with the Democrats and yet not quite fully in love with the Republicans, incapable of counting on social mobility, and watching helplessly as their children fall victim to drugs and obesity, Trump's supporters, like Arendt's masses, "grew out of the fragments of a highly atomized society whose competitive structure and concomitant loneliness of the individual had been held in check only through membership in a class." But as unions and working-class solidarity have begun to crumble, "it is only natural that these masses, in the first helplessness of the experience, have tended toward an especially violent nationalism, to which mass leaders have yielded against their own instincts and purposes for purely demagogic reasons."[39] In their poisonous combination of isolation and rage, those who see Donald Trump as their savior are acting out rather than acting. Their pain is the cause of their politics. It is my sense that the three authors I am discussing here, Hochschild, Moreton, and Cramer, wish to add texture to the popular stereotype of angry white voters who routinely vote Republican, and they are to be commended for trying to do so. But the way the very people they studied talked leaves me pessimistic about both their faith and their humanity.

In paying so much attention to Arendt, I am not suggesting that because there is so much mass anger loose in the land that the United States is about to turn totalitarian; this is not a "fascism is just around the corner" argument. But I am saying that the theory of mass society was dismissed a bit too quickly, even by some of the most insightful of the postwar liberals themselves. If the election of Donald Trump proves anything, it is that the winding down of a long postwar period of relative peace and prosperity should prompt us to think differently about our politics than we did in the years after World War II. In such a context, Daniel Bell's caution about the theory of mass society seems more hopeful than analytic, while Dwight Macdonald's critique of Masscult-Midcult seems more insightful than comic. Mass society may not have been relevant for their times, but it certainly seems to be for ours.

The theory of mass society, for one thing, helps us understand one special oddity of the Trump years: the indifference so many Trump supporters feel about how truly unsuited for democracy Trump's approach to politics really is. Mass society is not a place of conspicuous protest, left-wing or right-wing. A movement ruled by mass emotions is characterized by anomie rather than by energy; as much as the residents of mass society complain, and they complain endlessly, they wait to be acted upon by others rather than activate themselves. If for some of his voters, Trump can do wrong, that is because they lack any clear sense of what he might do right. To speak of the success or failure of his presidency is to use a language alien to his appeal. What his supporters want most is to see Trump in action, insulting his critics on Twitter, especially those who are African American, professional football players, or both; saying wildly inappropriate things about other leaders, especially women; and appearing constantly on the news, even while denigrating the media for covering the news. The point is always the appearance of movement: Arendt described this phenomenon as "the perpetual-motion mania of totalitarian movements which can remain in power so long as they keep moving and set everything around them in motion."[40]

Because mass society lacks energy and initiative, furthermore, its most immediate threat is not authoritarianism but anarchism. "The term masses," Arendt wrote, "applies only where we deal with people who either because of their sheer numbers, indifference, or both cannot be integrated into any organization based on a common interest, into political parties or municipal governments or professional organizations or trade unions."[41] When authoritarianism comes about, in other words, it is often preceded by radical libertarianism. A distrust of all collective action is necessary before collective action can become all-consuming. The leader offers the glue that the crowd lacks.

Inasmuch as they lack glue, it cannot be a surprise that so many of those attracted to right-wing nationalism express their dissatisfaction in libertarian terms. "I am so for capitalism and free enterprise," a respondent named Madonna tells Hochschild. "I hate the word 'regulate.' I don't want the size of my Coke bottle or type of lightbulb regulated. The American Dream is not due to socialism or the EPA. Sure, I want clean air and water," she adds, "but I trust our system to assure it."[42] The core ideological principle of these individuals is to get rid of regulations in all areas of life: they do not want to sugarcoat their words to please racial minorities, they want to drive their ATVs wherever they please, they distrust outsiders, they are of course desperate to hold on to their guns, and they certainly do not want to be told who can live next door. They may feel as if they are strangers in their own land, but this feeling is relieved by keeping strangers from other lands at a respectful distance. They have a one-way focus on citizenship: they want leaders to symbolically satisfy their emotional needs, but they do not want to participate in any discussions about what it might take to lessen their resentments or turn them into a positive force. Hochschild's respondents seem to have no interest in her and her Berkeley-centered world, even if she shows concern for theirs. Neither reform nor reaction is their cause. Simply hating government is. It is only in such a way that an individual can at one and the same time be a libertarian distrustful of the state and an authoritarian looking favorably upon it.

If there is one basic political truth these resentful Americans fail to recognize, it is that extreme libertarianism is a prelude to extreme authoritarianism, the very point that so many of the theorists of mass society tried to make. It is when the mediating institutions crumble, as Kornhauser argued, that anarchism and authoritarianism meet on terms favorable to both. In Arendt's terms, mass society can be said to exist when the elite and the mob form an alliance against the middle. Perhaps President Trump's ties with shady financial figures both in New York City and in Moscow, a real-life version of the Brecht/Weill *Rise and Fall of the City of Mahagonny*, would have come as no surprise to Arendt. The threat posed by Donald Trump is not that he will go back on his promises but that he will carry them out. Fortunately for American democracy, he seems to lack the discipline to ensure that he means what he said. Like his followers, he has no overriding cause either.

Prior to authoritarianism, the danger such radical libertarianism poses is one of too much democracy. Today's right-wing authoritarians take a highly simplified ideology and try to impose it on a world that has become more mobile and complex, a process that is bound to rile Americans up while leaving them feeling angry, abandoned, and dislocated. There is, however, an alternative: the people and their leaders can, in becoming more mature, accept, and even celebrate, the new world around them for its variety, diversity, and cosmopolitanism. Neither at the moment seems prepared to do so: the people remain too resentful and the leaders too opportunistic. And so we really do seem to be living in something resembling mass society, in which the people, as Arendt put it, are "deprived, not of the right to freedom but of the right to action: not of the right to think whatever they please but of the right to opinion."[43] Only in a democracy as open as America's could there be such a proliferation of people with closed minds.

Authoritarianism may well arrive at some point in the future, helped along the way by the paucity of resistance against its first steps. For now, however, Americans have an authoritarian personality in the presidency, not yet an authoritarian leader; our government is too sprawling and decentralized to be taken over all at once. This was not the situation facing the mature liberals: they already knew what authoritarianism in power could mean by looking at Europe, and it never meant anything pretty. Our danger is not that mass society has already arrived, although there are many indications that it is coming. It is the hint offered during the Trump years that if it did, a significant number of Americans, having been inoculated by Trump's words and deeds, would not care all that much. If Trump finds himself somehow reelected in 2020, we will know that the fears of mass society held by so many German writers in the 1930s and 1940s were not amiss.

The longest essay in Daniel Bell's *The New American Right* was by the sociologist Seymour Martin Lipset, and it contained the germ of a concept for which he would become famous: working-class authoritarianism. "The lower a person is in socioeconomic status or educational attainment," Lipset wrote, "the more likely he is to support McCarthy, favor restrictions on civil liberties, and back a 'get tough' policy with the Communist states."[44] Turning generations of left-wing scholarship and advocacy on their heads, Lipset was suggesting that Marx's "dictatorship of the proletariat" might turn out to be a dictatorship all right, but one more likely to be associated with what some now call the Alt Right. Searching for an explanation of why working-class voters were becoming more conservative, however, Lipset was somewhat lost. He and his colleagues were much given to the idea that a decline in a group's relative social status fuels its attraction to the right, but the working classes already had low social status. And so Lipset instead focused on smaller social forces: Catholic workers, for example, were likely to turn more conservative because the Catholic Church was so often at war with the Communist parties in Europe. His concept was provocative, to say the least, but the analysis was weak.

Lipset was nonetheless unwilling to let the concept of working-class authoritarianism lapse, and so when he published his award-winning book *Political Man* in 1960, he included a major chapter on the subject, with a significant adjustment in his analysis. Earlier in the book Lipset had discussed, briefly, the leading works in the theory of mass society, including Arendt's. Whether or not reading those works was the cause of his change in perspective, his analysis of working-class authoritarianism was now filled with themes from that literature. In language that no social scientist would dare use today, Lipset wrote that among the causes of the working classes' distrust of democracy were "low education, low participation in political or voluntary organizations of any type, little reading, isolated occupations, economic insecurity, authoritarian family patterns." Solitary, lacking job stability, leading lives filled with frustration and aggression, members of the working class were not only becoming authoritarian, he wrote; they will in difficult times "choose the least complex alternative." "All of these characteristics," he concluded, "produce a tendency to view politics and personal relations in black-and-white terms, a desire for immediate action, an impatience with talk and discussion, a lack of interest in organizations which have a long-range perspective and a readiness to follow leaders who offer a demonological interpretation of the evil forces (either religious or political) which are conspiring against him."[45] By no means were workers the only class attracted to the right, but the fact that they were deepened the problems faced by liberal democracies. Rising standards of living and more access to education might change the picture, Lipset concluded, but any such developments lay in the future.

That future, alas, has arrived, and it does not show much decrease in the forms of working-class authoritarianism; in one striking finding, researchers Ariel Malka and Yphtach Lelkes learned that half of the Republicans in this country believe that the 2020 election should be postponed so long as the problem of voter fraud, which in reality does not exist, is not solved.[46] Since so many Republican voters these days are working class, more particularly working class and white, and since so many Republicans are supporting an authoritarian president, Lipset could not have been proven more correct.

Nonetheless, for social scientists of a leftist bent, no other concept was greeted with as much disagreement as Lipset's key idea. In a typical critique, sociologists S. M. Miller and Frank Riessman responded that "no class has a monopoly on pro- or anti-democratic attitudes" and that Lipset ignored the conditions under which members of other classes might also turn in an authoritarian direction.[47] Their article set the tone for an emerging consensus that Lipset and his colleagues should be added to the ranks of former radicals now rethinking their positions and moving to the center—or even to the right.[48] The Socialist hope that the workers would lead the movement against capitalism was so entrenched on the left, including the non-Marxist left, that Lipset really did appear as a heretic. He broke one of the left's most sacred taboos, the one associated with the power and potential of the working class, and was treated by many, for a while including myself, as outside the pale. Lose hope in the working class, was the message back then, and lose all hope.

Today, Lipset—and not his critics—comes out looking far better. Even before Trump's election, Tom Edsall of the *New York Times* had outlined the major features of what he called "the great Democratic inversion."[49] When Lipset was writing, working-class voters, even if listing toward authoritarianism, still tended to vote Democratic, and wealthy individuals, even while becoming more liberal on social and cultural issues, still tended to vote Republican. The great inversion has changed all that. Now it is the Democrats who tend to win in the wealthy suburbs, where the culture leans cosmopolitan, especially in the Northeast, while the Republicans are attracting disaffected working-class whites in the heartland. The great inversion suggests that Lipset should be viewed as more a prophet than a turncoat. No one from his era, I believe, could ever have predicted Trump, but it was possible to predict his following, and Lipset did just that.

Perhaps the single greatest contribution to an understanding of American politics made by the generation of Arendt and Lipset—along with the Frankfurt school's Theodor Adorno and his attempt to measure authoritarian proclivities through what he called his F-Scale—will prove to be their willingness to disabuse people of the notion that those at the bottom of the economic scale necessarily hold the key to limiting the power of those at the top. Endorsing this idea does not mean leaving the left and joining the right; Lipset, although often accused of neoconservatism, never did. Just because Marx viewed the proletariat as a revolutionary class does not mean that everyone else must. There are many sources of progress in America that lie outside the concerns and culture of the working class. Identifying them, and then finding ways to unify them, may make more sense to the left of the future than looking for social change from a class that prefers its politicians as coarse as they are crude.

There are two threats to the future health of democracy, and there are two proposed solutions, one for each. Both the Republican Party and a significant group of conservative pundits view the threat to democracy in quantitative terms. Too many people vote, they believe, even if they do not always say so explicitly, and the solution is to make it more difficult for them to do so. Proponents of a classic conservative vision of government by the proper few, these restrictionists are fully aware that the history of democracy is the history of the extension of the franchise, and they want that history to stop. Imposing requirements on suffrage, they argue, will help guarantee that only those who have a stake in public policy will shape it. Democrats, in their view, have created a corrupt system in which all kinds of benefits are offered to the poor and downtrodden only to insure that the poor and downtrodden vote Democratic. This is a cynical cycle, they insist, and it must be met by decisive action, even if such actions remind people of the notorious methods once used to prevent black voting in the South, such as poll taxes and the registration requirement.

Although sponsored by conservatives, such ways of restricting the vote depend upon a liberal conception of the polity. Voting restrictionists assume, as liberal theory does, that people act according to their interests. Society, in this view, is still organized along class lines, and the object of voting restrictions is to make it easier for one class to dominate while disenfranchising another (or others); the politics around voter restriction, one can say, is Marxism in reverse. Voting restriction received official presidential recognition when President Trump created a panel to examine voting irregularities and appointed such prominent restrictionists as Kris Kobach and Hans von Spakovsky to it. These individuals, in line with their party, insist, against all evidence, that all too much fraud exists at the ballot box. In reality, their goal, and it was hardly a secret, was to use the concept of voting fraud to make it more difficult for minorities and Democrats to exercise the franchise. In January 2018, President Trump dissolved the panel, and not long after that state courts began to declare extreme partisan gerrymandering unconstitutional. The era of quantitative restricting of suffrage may be coming to an end, although adherents to such restrictions are unlikely ever to give up.

But what if the problems facing our democracy grow out of mass society rather than class society? There certainly is evidence that this could well be the case. No longer is voting determined by a person's place in a world of organizational density, such as by membership in a labor union or by working for a large corporation. In theory, voters are free agents calculating alternative promises from the candidates. In reality, they bear a disturbing resemblance to the mass man pictured by Dwight Macdonald and other critics of mass society. Finding a solution to the qualitative problem of the way we vote is much more difficult than finding one for the quantitative one. If we are to improve the quality of our democratic life, we will have to ask whether the enormous responsibility that democracy imposes on its citizens—to take with mature seriousness the decision about how we are governed—is adequately addressed. This is not a terrain in which liberals generally feel comfortable.

Because they were so familiar with the theory of mass society, the mature liberals of the 1950s were far more aware than scholars today of the impact that immature voting can have on democratic politics. In the rich intellectual environment in which they wrote, civics was actually taught in high school (though one assumes not too well), and political scientists took the health of democracy as one of their major concerns: Robert A. Dahl and E. E. Schattshneider certainly did, and even an economist, Joseph Schumpeter, joined the fray.[50] (Fortunately, that trend has continued, as the recent work of Harvard's Steven Levitsky and Daniel Ziblatt shows.[51]) The mature liberals were part of this movement. One of the powerful critiques of the way Americans treat their one major obligation of citizenship, suffrage, came in 1950 when David Riesman and his collaborators published *The Lonely Crowd*. "How is it possible," they wrote in some bewilderment, "to live in America, speak and read English, own a radio, without ever having heard of the Marshall Plan, Henry Wallace and even—as in one of our interviews with a high school senior—without being sure what party Truman belongs to?" The expansion of suffrage, in theory, assumed that "the electoral process would change and general political activity be heightened and improved," but instead it has produced enormous cynicism, since the "other-directed" person, to use Riesman's concept, is "essentially passive—a self-conscious puppet tolerantly watching and making sure that the strings that move him do not touch his heart."[52] Indifference and apathy are strengthened because both are subject to the group pressure that other-direction requires.

The McCarthy period, which began just after *The Lonely Crowd* was published, reinforced the idea that America, as Hofstadter put it, "suffers . . . from an implacable dislike and suspicion of all constituted authority," and that its right wing "is constituted out of a public that simply cannot arrive at a psychological modus vivendi with authority, cannot reconcile itself to that combination of acceptance and criticism which the democratic process requires of the relationship between the leaders and the led."[53] But the solution the mature liberals proposed—greater reliance on elites, such as in England—is not available to us today. That is why it is so incumbent on those who worry about the state of our democracy to dig deeper, a task I will try to undertake in the final chapter of this book. We cannot say of any society that we should look somewhere else to see how much better democracy works over there, not at a time when, according to *The Economist*, democracy is increasingly in trouble everywhere.[54] No other democracy is led by anyone like Donald Trump. But that does not mean that other democracies find themselves crisis-free.

4
FROM CONSPIRACY TO IRONY

The best-known words ever to pass the lips of Senator Joseph McCarthy concerned his discovery of "a conspiracy on a scale so immense as to dwarf any previous venture in the history of man, . . . a conspiracy of infamy so black that, when it is finally exposed, its principals shall be forever deserving of the maledictions of all honest men."[1] Readers new to McCarthy's methods may be surprised to learn that the person alleged to be at the center of this dangerously unprecedented conspiracy was no Communist, left-winger, or subversive. He was, in fact, one of the most distinguished Americans of his (or any other) time: General George Catlett Marshall, US Army Chief of Staff during World War II, head of both the State and Defense Departments after the war, and the person after whom the plan to help Europe rebuild was named. Anyone who believes that Donald Trump is the first successful politician to tell grossly exaggerated lies about very prominent people has not studied the McCarthy period; for McCarthy, the more respected the target, the more merciless the attack.

In the right-wing mind of McCarthy's time, Marshall's was only one of a host of conspiracies said to be selling out the United States. Moderate Republican senator Thomas Kuchel of California, himself smeared by charges that he was arrested by the Los Angeles police for committing homosexual acts, received mail claiming that 35,000 Chinese Communist troops wearing powder-blue uniforms were about to invade San Diego; a Russian colonel was in charge of the US Army, Navy, and Air Force; and the United Nations was running a guerilla-warfare campaign against America from the swamps of the state of Georgia. All such assertions, according to Richard Hofstadter, "illustrate the central preoccupation of the paranoid style—the existence of a vast, insidious, preternaturally effective international conspiratorial network designed to perpetuate acts of the most fiendish character."[2] Supporting the campaign of Barry Goldwater in 1964, the right-wing activist Phyllis Schlafly published her best-selling book *A Choice Not an Echo*.[3] Her title was well chosen: the choice facing the radical right back then was between fact and fiction, and most of its adherents chose fiction.

Hofstadter's analysis of the conspiratorial mind had two purposes. One, as befitting a historian, was to show that conspiracy theories have always been with us. To this end, Hofstadter reminded his readers of the attacks on the Bavarian Illuminati in eighteenth-century Europe that attracted numerous followers in this country; the persistent campaign against the Masons and their secret rites and rituals; and anti-Catholicism, which, as he wittily put it, "has always been the pornography of the Puritan."[4]

Examples from the past were plentiful, but Hofstadter, secondly, did not want his readers to come away with the impression that the conspiracies emanating from Joseph McCarthy and the radical right were just reiterations of long-established themes. "The villains of the modern right," he wrote, "are much more vivid than those of their paranoid predecessors." Previous conspiratorial thinking had confined itself to the charge that the country was under attack, but now the focus was worldwide, as global events, including those in China and Korea, "have given the contemporary right-wing paranoid a vast theatre for his imagination, full of rich and proliferating detail, replete with realistic clues and undeniable proofs of the validity of his views." It was very much like war. "The enemy is clearly delineated: he is a perfect model of malice, a kind of amoral superman: sinister, ubiquitous, powerful, cruel, sensual, luxury loving."[5] The powers of the paranoid's enemies were vast, and their insights and strategies brilliant. Until now, the moment when we have for the first time brought publicity to their evil deeds, they have won pretty much every war they fought.

In spite of all this, Hofstadter nonetheless believed that the paranoid style demonstrated "how much political leverage can be got out of the animosities and passions of a small minority." Because of its minority status, conspiratorial thinking was for him more an indicator of a serious potential crisis in our politics than it was an ongoing, everyday aspect of American political life. Perhaps if exposed by serious scholarship, he may well have reasoned, conspiratorial thinking would never gain a permanent foothold. Hofstadter suggested of the paranoid that "circumstances often deprive him of exposure to events that might enlighten him." There was, it would seem, a chance, even if slight, that the influence of paranoia on America would abate.[6]

Has such an abatement taken place since Hofstadter wrote? The most extensive effort to answer this question, *American Conspiracy Theories*, by Joseph Usinscki and Joseph Parent, suggests that it has.[7] Yet Usinscki and Parent's research was undertaken well before Donald Trump's success, which was due in part to Trump's early and persistent use of one of the most pernicious conspiracy theories of our time: that our first black president had not been born in the United States. Trump's victory, furthermore, was fueled by a variety of other conspiracy claims. Inoculation causes autism. Thousands of New Jersey Muslims celebrated the attack on 9/11. The shooting of elementary-school children in Sandy Hook, Connecticut, never happened but was staged for the media. Hillary Clinton suffered from an unknown disease, perhaps Parkinson's. A DC pizza parlor served as a front for a child-abuse sex ring. An unsolved attempted robbery involving a young Democratic activist named Seth Rich was in reality an execution ordered by Clinton to silence the man responsible for the release of Democratic National Committee emails. Justice Scalia was smothered to death. Ted Cruz's father was involved in the Kennedy assassination. Trump and his supporters pushed these and other claims. Some were successful, others were not.

The sheer number of these conspiracies raises the question of whether all this is just a continuation of previous patterns in our history, revised to account for new events, or whether it signals a qualitative change in conspiratorial thinking from the outer edges of the political world to its very center in the White House. The former possibility suggests that we are living through a temporary abnormality and that matters will return to their normal, that is, nonconspiratorial, thinking given enough time. The latter suggests that after Trump, American politics will never again be the same, that conspiracy, as they say, is the new normal. Future developments will help answer these questions, but until the future arrives, there is good reason to believe that conspiracy theorizing has dug deeper roots in our political culture these days than it did when McCarthy's attacks were so prominent.

Social scientists have begun to carry out extensive research into conspiratorial thinking, and their findings are not reassuring to those who believe that rationality is a necessity of a well-functioning political system. Half of the American people believe in one or another conspiracy theory, political scientists have found, and the greatest predictor of whether they do is not related to conservatism or ignorance but instead to "magical thinking" in general.[8] Given the way conspiracy theories influence each other, it cannot be surprising that 59 percent of Americans believe that more than one person was involved in the Kennedy assassination, 55 percent that a similar conspiracy took place when Martin Luther King Jr. was shot, and 31 percent that foul play was involved in the death of Princess Diana.[9] These kinds of findings can be dismissed as trivial curiosities, no more important to our politics than the latest issue of *People*, but even on matters central to the future of the planet, such as global warming, conspiracy theories abound: an especially definitive study showed that when people were exposed to a propaganda film denying global warming, their questioning of the science behind the idea increased.[10] Even the Holy Grail of all conspiracy theories—the denial or the de-Judification of the Holocaust—found itself on the political agenda when the Trump administration issued a statement on Holocaust Remembrance Day in 2017 that did not mention the Jewish people.

How can we determine whether conspiratorial thinking has

increased or decreased since the 1950s, especially when surveys in those days either did not exist or were untrustworthy? One measure is that Joseph McCarthy's conspiracy theories did not put him in the White House, while Donald Trump's did. And whether or not conspiratorial thinking has increased, technology and the political culture of the United States have changed in dramatic ways since McCarthy's era, making whatever conspiratorial thinking exists both more prominent and more pronounced. Today's political paranoia, in short, is spread by new technologies, purveyed by new personalities, and preoccupied with new themes, yet all of it is done in the same spirit of malevolence that so bothered Hofstadter and the other mature liberals.

The Internet and social media, of course, make it possible for conspiracies to spread rapidly. Joe McCarthy and his radical right collaborators were quite good at using the media of their time, but not in their wildest fantasies could they have imagined a device that would get their thoughts out to the world in the blink of an eye. Americans received a glimpse of the future of conspiratorial thinking when they learned the extent to which the Russians had relied upon such media as Facebook to spread stories about gun control, Black Lives Matter, and other election issues, thereby injecting themselves into an American election campaign. When forms of media with almost no checks become globalized, anything, literally, goes.

Relatedly, new technologies have also accelerated the process by which subgroups of like-minded believers form and sustain themselves. One of the leading researchers into conspiracy theories is Kate Starbird, a professor of computer science. Starbird and her students collected tweets in the aftermath of such man-made crisis events as the Boston Marathon bombing, the Sandy Hook shooting, and the Orlando nightclub attack, revealing an "alternative narrative ecosystem" based not on mainstream reporting but on a self-perpetuating rumor machine in which "alternative media domains may be acting as a breeding ground for the transmission of conspiratorial ideas."[11] With the power of social media at hand, conspiracies breed new conspiracies that then intensify the cycle all over again. Nothing seems to please the conspiratorial mind quite like sitting in front of one's computer and sharing one's special knowledge with the cognoscenti, wherever they can be found. Conspiracy theorists used to spin webs. Now they rely on one.

Not only does the Web help spread conspiracy theories, it makes it more difficult to combat them. Cass Sunstein, a law professor who served in the Obama administration as the director of the White House Office of Information and Regulatory Affairs, has preoccupied himself with this issue.[12] Two broad kinds of social problems are associated with societies given to conspiracy theories, Sunstein argues. One, as Starbird found, is that people who communicate only with each other do not interact with people outside their group, a tendency that works against the importance of interpersonal communication in liberal democracy. The second is what Sunstein calls the power of crippled epistemologies, the idea that people do not know nearly as much as they think and that much of what they do know is false. (The Web being what it is, Sunstein's concept was quickly subject to extensive criticism the moment it was proposed.) For Sunstein, the problem in high conspiracy societies is not low information; conspiracy fans have plenty of information, and some of it is even correct. The problem is that mechanisms for correcting false information do not work; the conspiratorially inclined, faced with a conflict between their beliefs and actual reality, will reinterpret the latter to uphold the former, and not the other way around. Sunstein includes reflections on how governments might combat conspiracy theories by encouraging "cognitive diversity" among those who lack it, but his suggestions, such as relying on infiltrators to encourage minor conspiracies in order to possess the credibility of countering more dangerous ones, just suggest how difficult it is to stop the ways in which self-referential subgroups reinforce their peculiar interpretation of the world around them.

McCarthy raged against Communists during one of the greatest periods of scientific and technological accomplishment in our history. In the first five years of the 1950s, Jonas Salk rushed to complete the work on his polio vaccine. The double helix was discovered. Type 1 and type 2 diabetes were named. Cigarette smoking and high levels of cholesterol were linked to heart disease. The first organ transplant took place. Color television first became available. And the Diner's Club Card made its debut. The enormous prestige accorded science and technology in the 1950s was premised on the assumption that certain things were true, others false, and proper training could help detect the difference between them. McCarthy could exploit doubts, but at some point his charges were capable of being disproved.

We now live at a time when "crippled epistemologies" are the rule rather than exception, because a suspicion toward experts has spread rapidly throughout America. The McCarthy period involved a disagreement over opinion. Ours involves a disagreement over facts. It hardly matters how many published articles in scientific journals disprove any link between inoculation and autism or how robust is the finding that fossil-fuel consumption leads to higher levels of carbon dioxide; critics will remain critics. When science is distrusted, indeed when it comes under direct attack, conspiracy theories are given greater credibility. If we cannot agree that the breaking off of an Antarctic iceberg as large as the state of Delaware is something we should worry about, how could we ever disprove that the US government is engaged in a secret plot to take away the guns of God-fearing ordinary Americans or that 9/11 was an inside job? In the past decade or two, we have witnessed a fairly severe politicization of science in which expertise and data-driven conclusions are increasingly suspect.[13]

The most obvious consequence of this distrust of expertise is what the journalist Chris Mooney has called the Republican war on science, an effort to refute or ignore any scientific method or finding that does not conform to the party's ideological agenda.[14] At one level, this is not new: Hofstadter, after all, wrote extensively about William Jennings Bryan, and Bryan, besides his populism, was widely known for his refusal to accept Darwinism. What is surprising is that so many years after the Scopes trial, critics of evolution still possess sufficient influence to shape public policy at the state level. For example, Tennessee, where the Scopes trial took place, passed a law in 2012 giving public school teachers the right to teach explanations of human development other than the Darwinian one. This is science by and for populists:

the idea that evolution is just one theory and ought to be taught along with other theories sounds fair to all sides in a controversy, but all it does is perpetuate ignorance. The overall conclusion to be drawn from the dramatic levels of scientific distrust and suspicion of expertise is that the very phenomenon Hofstadter studied, anti-intellectualism, is on the increase. And according to one study, it actually is.[15]

Just as populism comes in left and right forms, so do conspiracy theories, and this too constitutes a difference between the McCarthy period and our own era. Hofstadter and his colleagues wrote about the radical right because that was where all the perversities of politics at their time seemed to reside. But in the aftermath of Donald Trump's successful reliance on conspiratorial thinking, his opponents have been trying the same thing. Was Andrew Breitbart, the founder of Breitbart News, murdered by the Russians so that Steve Bannon could take over the organization? Louise Mensch, a former British Tory MP now living in New York who appeals to a left-wing audience, thinks so. When questioned intensively by the BBC, Mensch claimed that her views did not involve any reporting but were simply an assertion of her belief, as if that resolved all questions.[16] A Twitter aficionado, Mensch can be counted on to provide at least one conspiracy a day to her devoted fans. Here is one:

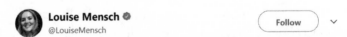

My sources say the death penalty, for espionage, being considered for @StevenKBannon. I am pro-life and take no pleasure in reporting this.

4:54 AM - 19 Jul 2017

Mensch has had her five minutes of fame: the *New York Times* published two op-eds by her defending Brexit and offering ideas about who the congressional investigators of Trump's Russia connections should call as witnesses (and what they should be asked).[17] Such recognition, I imagine, is what conspiracy theorists live for, since, to the best of my knowledge, Steve Bannon, although no longer working for the Trump administration, is alive and well.

Trump's connection with Russia, a society given to secrecy, has furthermore created a wide-open field for leftist conspiracy theorists to make one wild claim after another; nearly all of them, including the assertion that Trump was being blackmailed over his "pee pee tape," can conveniently be found on a website called the Palmer Report.[18] (The "pee pee tape" refers to the rumor, said to be contained in a secret British intelligence dossier in the possession of former British spy Christopher Steele, that Trump had paid prostitutes to pee on a hotel bed in Moscow once slept in by Barack Obama.) Five or so years ago, I would have argued that there was nothing on the left similar to the paranoia on the right, and even today the sheer quantity of right-wing paranoia surely overwhelms anything on the other end of the spectrum. Still I also think it fair to say that the general suspicion of truth characterizing America today has made it possible for conspiracy theories to sprout wherever political unhappiness can be found.

One aspect of left-wing conspiracy theories is especially noteworthy: if one stands on the left side of the spectrum, what the Republicans are doing is sufficiently hostile to democracy to require no exaggeration. Had I been writing during the McCarthy period, for example, and suggested that future Republicans would refuse to vote on a nominee for the Supreme Court until their party was in power, or that the same party would work strenuously to deny Democrats the right to vote in various states, or that the Russians would play a prominent role in an American political campaign, I would have been dismissed as no more serious than the John Birch Society and its belief that President Eisenhower was a Communist agent. Winning an election does not make conspiracy theorizing go away. On the contrary, governing encourages conspiratorial talk to rally the base, just as it serves in helping prepare for the next campaign. We seem to be in the era of the permanent conspiracy theory.

A glance back at how the McCarthy period ended suggests an additional reason for concluding that our time is especially ripe for conspiracy thinking. McCarthy reached his end when he attacked one of the more respected American institutions, the US Army: the prestige of the military was so great in those days that McCarthy committed political suicide with his vendetta against it. Being a military officer is still a highly prestigious position, but after numerous defeats and stalemates abroad, and after plentiful examples of corruption, wasteful spending, and sexual harassment, much of that polish has worn off. (Today's officer closest to George C. Marshall in accomplishments is David Petraeus, who was wounded by his release of military secrets to a woman with whom he was having an affair. The prestige of generals took a further hit when Donald Trump's chief of staff General John Kelly publicly lied about what had taken place at an FBI ceremony, never apologized for it, went on to attack "Dreamers," those noncitizens brought to the United States as children, and at first defended the domestic abuser Rob Porter, the former staff secretary for President Trump.) Both parties still habitually support greater spending on the military, and serving in the military still carries prestige. Yet today it is possible to imagine a career politician attacking the military and remaining in office, as Republican senator Rand Paul has done. McCarthy's attack came in an era when the military still operated with an aura of invincibility. Attack a prominent general today, and you might find yourself lionized by the Alt Right and the Alt Left, which these days calls itself Antifa.

During the McCarthy period, finally, political polarization was nothing like what it has since become. Loyalty to one's political party was not considered a virtue in those years. In 1956, for example, John F. Kennedy wrote a prize-winning book celebrating those who were not.[19] We should not be surprised, then, that some of leading opponents of Joe McCarthy, such as Senators Margaret Chase Smith of Maine and Ralph Flanders of Vermont, were members of his own party. They knew that opposition from within the party would be far more effective in checking McCarthy than opposition from Democrats, since the latter was only to be expected. By choosing country over party, they improved the political health of the former.

Today party loyalty has become more like a Mafia code of honor: you remain silent when scandal appears in your party or you will pay dearly. It is possible for a few Republican senators to defy their president, such as Susan Collins of Maine, Jeff Flake and John McCain of Arizona, and Bob Corker of Tennessee. But none of those have been persistent critics, and all of them have at times followed their party's line. This is why Mitch McConnell, the majority leader of the US Senate, can count on party loyalty much more than Republican congressional leaders in the 1950s could. In the 1950s, political scientists discussed the idea of parties based on the British system, where loyalty was strong. Now we actually have a situation like that, and democracy appears to be even less safe now than it was then. Party loyalty sounds like such a good thing, but when it facilitates the authoritarianism of the demagogue, it becomes quite the opposite. If there exists a moment in which congressional Republicans stand up against Donald Trump, it has not yet come.

"We are all sufferers from history," Hofstadter concluded in his essay on the paranoid style, "but the paranoid is a double sufferer, since he is afflicted not only by the real world, with the rest of us, but by his fantasies as well."[20] In his own way, Hofstadter was far too optimistic. Let the fantasist attract a large-enough following, and the fantasy will no longer be an illness from which one suffers but a key to secret knowledge that offers solidarity and significance. Paranoia is no longer an odd by-product of the way we do politics in America. It has become, like fund-raising and advertising, a routine aspect of campaigns and governance. Hofstadter wrote about the paranoid "style." Today we should be more worried by the paranoid "substance."

In their permanent distrust of government, Americans have learned to take what their leaders proclaim in their speeches or announce in their policy statements with a grain of salt. This in itself is a positive attribute, at least for democratic politics. A deep strain of untruth, after all, has played out in this country since at least the administration of Lyndon Johnson, which lied so much about the progress of the war in Vietnam. Richard Nixon at first denied any personal involvement in the scandal that became known as Watergate. Jimmy Carter unrealistically told the American people he would never lie to them. Ronald Reagan denied sending weapons to anti-Communist groups in Nicaragua financed by selling arms to Iran. Bill Clinton claimed that he never had sex with that woman. George Bush and Dick Cheney falsely claimed that Saddam Hussein possessed weapons of mass destruction. And, just when we thought that Bush and Cheney were untoppable in their sheer mendacity, Donald Trump topped them all with lies too numerous to count. In the face of repeated untruths, a willingness to question what political leaders claim has become a requirement of serious American citizenship.

Because under the Trump administration lying is a daily occurrence, public vigilance seems on the rise as well. But just as there are many ways to lie, there are also many ways to protect the truth. Roughly speaking, the American public has two major forms of such protection: skepticism and suspicion. The former has positive consequences for democracy and ought to be encouraged. The latter is dangerous to democracy and ought to be avoided.

Skepticism is humanistic, insightful, detached, and humble. The skeptic assumes innocence until guilt is proven and is more inclined to ask questions than to repeat answers. Skepticism encourages distance; we must know what we are fighting before we fight the wrong enemy. It is also accompanied by humor, as in the novels of Mark Twain or Muriel Spark. Skepticism is the normal reaction of those acting thoughtfully. Certainly the mature liberals themselves were skeptics; their approach to politics required that they establish a certain distance from what John Kenneth Galbraith called "the conventional wisdom" of the time.[21] This was an especially important quality in a period of mass hysteria, which the McCarthy period clearly was: while McCarthy was attacking Marshall, some thinking Americans would soon be attending Arthur Miller's play *The Crucible*, the subject of which was the real witch-hunt that had taken place in Salem, Massachusetts, in 1692. This atmosphere of skepticism explains why the more left wing of the New York intellectuals, when starting a magazine in 1954, called their effort *Dissent*, and why one of its founders, Irving Howe, wrote an article that year titled "This Age of Conformity."[22]

Suspicion, by contrast, provides the natural habitat for the conspiracy theorist. It begins and ends with distrust. The suspicious are always on the qui vive, certain that calm times will soon become perilous ones. Suspicion is dark, covert, and dangerous. Suspicious people judge first and seek evidence, if at all, afterward. They are also marked by a lack of curiosity: one has no need to ask questions if one already knows the answers. Instead of humor, the suspicious prefer sarcasm, the heavier, generally, the better. *Suspicion* was the name of one of Alfred Hitchcock's greatest films; *Skepticism* could never have been. To live in an age of suspicion, as the journalist James A. Weschler called the McCarthy period, is to live under a cloud that includes both the hunter and the hunted.[23] Suspicion is always in a hurry: we must act and we must act now, before the enemy becomes unstoppable.

The very nature of what we are up against makes the conspiracy hunter very suspicious. Conspirators always make their plans in dingy basements, never in air-conditioned lofts. Those who hunt them are not afraid to copy their methods, lest those enemies obtain the upper hand. For all the vehemence of those with conspiratorial minds, ideology is of secondary importance to them—one reason some who joined the radical parties of the left later switched sides to join the radical parties of the right. Suspicion hates ambiguity. Although the suspicious find themselves in an antagonistic relationship with the state, they act as if they had all the powers of the state at their disposal: they are inquisitorial, absolutist, unforgiving, unabated, and unabashed. One might think they are in charge even when they are not.

One of the major tasks of the mature liberals was to search for a method that would provide them with the virtues of the skeptic without the vices of the suspicious. They found such a method in the nature of irony. For Daniel Bell, for example, the key terms of his group's outlook on the world would be "irony, paradox, ambiguity, and complexity."[24] Why did Bell put irony first? The answer lies in the writings of two of the mature liberals who were not social scientists: Lionel Trilling and Reinhold Niebuhr.

Like the conspiracist, the ironist believes that everything is not as it seems; in an essay on Jane Austen's *Mansfield Park*, for example,

Trilling wrote that irony "perceives the world through an awareness of its contradictions, paradoxes, and anomalies." But the ironist does this in a very different way than the conspiracist. Irony, especially in Austen's hands, is, Trilling insisted, a force for good. "To Jane Austen," he wrote, "irony does not mean, as it does to many, a moral detachment or the tone of superiority that goes with moral detachment." On the contrary, irony "is a method of comprehension" that "is partisan with generosity of spirit—it is on the side of 'life,' of 'affirmation.'" The detachment we attain through irony is not equivalent to the anger provided by conspiracy. It enables us to forgive frivolity and "is animated by an impulse to forgiveness."[25] This kind of irony accompanies a liberal temperament just as conspiracy does a reactionary one; it gives us a way of distancing ourselves from the world without rejecting it in toto.

Niebuhr was even more of an ironist then Trilling because, as a Christian, he understood that because we seek a better world while simultaneously being stained by original sin, the things we do will likely not have the effects we hope they will. For him, the effort to create utopia, so present in Marxism but also a feature of liberalism poorly understood, "generates more extravagant forms of political injustice and cruelty out of the pretentions of innocency than we have ever know in human history." America, because of the circumstances of its birth and development, was particularly prone to innocence. Watching our clumsy efforts to be all-powerful and omniscient, God can only laugh because, as George Frederick Handel famously set His words to music, "the people imagine a vain thing." America has a "deep layer of Messianic consciousness," Niebuhr wrote, which, when unleashed upon the world could put everyone in enormous danger. It is not that America's actions in the world express the tragic; if they did, they could not be Christian. What makes America such a fascinating experiment is more dialectical: its determination to do good combined with its frequent failures to actually do so. "The question for a nation, particularly for a very powerful nation, is whether the necessary exercise of its virtue in meeting ruthlessness and the impressive nature of its power will blind it to the ambiguity of all human virtues and competencies; or whether even a nation might have some residual awareness of the larger meanings of the drama of human existence beyond and above the immediate urgencies."[26]

In the years since these thinkers wrote, irony has continued to play an important role in liberal thinking, as in the work of the philosopher Richard Rorty. Rorty had his own personal connections with the mature liberals: his father, James, had coauthored a book arguing the McCarthy was insufficiently anti-Communist, and he figured in Lipset's contribution to *The New American Right* observing the uses Roy Cohn made of his Jewishness. Further, Rorty's grandfather Walter Rauschenbusch had had a complicated intellectual and personal relationship with Niebuhr. Unlike Niebuhr, Richard Rorty could never accept the proposition that there existed an all-powerful force whose commanding and authoritative words would settle disputes between human beings. The nature of our condition, by contrast, is that we must live in a time when proof, or what Rorty calls "the final vocabulary" under which we live, is unattainable. The ironist realizes that this is our condition and, for all its uncertainty, comes to accept its contingencies: "For the liberal ironist skill at imaginative identification does the work which the liberal metaphysician would like to have done by a specifically moral motivation—rationality, or the love of God, or the love of truth."[27] Literary criticism offers a better guide to how we ought to live that philosophical rigor because it analyzes case studies of the working of morality and gives us illustrative material to carry on our never-quite-resolvable disputes with others.

There is an interesting irony involved in how irony became so important for these thinkers. Appreciative of the depth of the humanities, the mature liberals were not quite on board with the revolution in the social sciences taking place in the years they wrote. They did admire those sociologists who shared their general outlook; Trilling, for example, wrote, with regard to *The Lonely Crowd*, that "no American novel of recent years has been able to give me the sense of the actuality of our society that I get from Mr. Riesman's book," in large part because Riesman's values were "paradoxes, ambiguities, anomalies, contradictions, and ironies." Riesman was, however, the exception. More generally these humanists had little or no respect for the positivistic social sciences; efforts to capture human identity in scientific form, in their view, were hopeless, if not immoral. "Sociology," Trilling wrote, "tends to use a language which must arouse antagonism in people who are at all sensitive to language,"[28] while Niebuhr expressed his criticism this way: "When political science is severed from its ancient rootage in the humanities and 'enriched' by the wisdom of the sociologists, psychologists and anthropologists, the result is frequently a preoccupation with minutiae which obscures the grand and tragic outlines of contemporary history, and offers vapid solutions for profound problems."[29] It is as if both writers somehow glimpsed a future in which their own work would come to seem archaic in contrast to the ambitious efforts of more scientific social scientists.

The irony here is that the thinker that led so many of these individuals to their respect for irony was precisely one of these sociologists, a man of great learning to be sure, but also one intent on making sociology more scientific. His name was Robert K. Merton and he also taught at Columbia and was close to Trilling and Hofstadter. One of his most famous articles, "The Unanticipated Consequences of Purposive Social Action," although published in 1936, well before McCarthy's time on the stage, anticipates the respect for the ironic developed by his colleagues: we try to do one thing, ran the thrust of his argument, only to discover that we wind up doing something else. "Merton's functional analysis," wrote the essayist Benjamin DeMott, "uncovered a way layered in ironies: good producing evil, evil producing good, a variety of evidence testifying that benign intention, in emergencies or otherwise, never insures favorable results." His objective, DeMott tells us, was exactly the same as Hofstadter's and almost the same as Trilling's: "an effort to subject Cant to cold-eyes scrutiny without obstructing potential moral progress." Although he was primarily neither an essayist nor a commentator on daily events, Merton's influence on his colleagues was enormous.

DeMott's summary of what these thinkers accomplished is the single best account of the achievements of mature liberalism:

> From this sense of mind—this love of the mind's disciplines and ambitions, its variousness and flexibility—grew the standard of discourse that was responsible for the country's last memorable moment of broadly based intellectual promise. In the voice of the elders—in their tone—two truths resound that deserve to live on a little longer, and our task is to find a language that will ensure their survival. One truth is that nothing can be done to ease injustice or oppression except with the aid of the flexible intelligence, the mobile imagination, and the will to self-sacrifice. The other truth, simpler and deeper and inexpressibly precious, is that honest shame is not to be mocked.[30]

As pleasing as it may be for us to believe that there are simple answers to complex problems, even a casual understanding of how the world actually works would force us into a deeper understanding of human beings and their societies. The mature liberals could never be progressive because the progressive mind is insufficiently mature.

There was also a conservative side to functional analysis as Merton conceived of it: if any institution or social practice functions well, why tamper with it? It may well have been this conservative instinct that led one of the most prolific of the mature liberals, Daniel Bell, to join the prominent neoconservative Irving Kristol in the editing of *The Public Interest*. Irony dominated the approach of that magazine from its founding in 1965 to its demise forty years later. Weary from the ideological struggles of their youth, those who wrote for the magazine believed that a moderate use of the findings of the social sciences could help us by avoiding social reforms that, guided by a radical ideology, might prove to be overambitious, wrong, or counterproductive. Bell left the magazine in 1973, rumored to be upset by its increasingly conservative direction. There is no doubt that the magazine overall was conservative, but I value its skepticism far more than its doctrine.

Daniel Patrick Moynihan, the assistant secretary of labor in both the Kennedy and Johnson administrations, wrote the first article in the first issue of *The Public Interest*, titled "The Professionalization of Reform."[31] That was not, however, his major accomplishment that year.

In March 1965 Moynihan also issued his famous report "The Negro Family: The Case for National Action."[32] The result was a national uproar, the first relatively recent outbreak of what would come to be called "political correctness." Moynihan, it was said, was blaming the victim. Because he focused on culture and not such structural factors as unemployment, he was charged and found guilty of arguing that we should do nothing to promote racial justice, a charge that doubled in intensity when, a few years later, Moynihan added the term "benign neglect" to our political vocabulary.[33]

Moynihan is certainly one of the most colorful of the mature liberals. It is not my intention here to pass judgment on the issues that made him so controversial, save to say that in recent years white families have been breaking down at a rate even more rapid than that he assigned to black families. Moynihan interests me for another reason. As both a thinker and a public official, he was caught between two contradictory roles. The issues with which Moynihan concerned himself as a policymaker were, literally, deadly serious: it would be difficult to find a problem more in need of attention in the 1960s, when one city after another was burning to the ground, than racial equality. As a thinker, however, Moynihan was strongly influenced by the ironic stance taken by his colleagues among the mature liberals, along with their great respect for the English language. Moynihan's main problem was that his skepticism offended those engaged with policies around which no sense of irony was permitted. His ability to write so well, his twinkle-in-the-eye style, led to Moynihan being attacked as much for how he expressed himself as for what he urged. Not only did "benign neglect" enter our political vocabulary but so did "tangle of pathologies," "There are some mistakes that only a person with a Ph.D. can make," "The central conservative truth is that it is culture, and not politics, that determines the success of a society" while "the central liberal truth is that politics can change a culture and save it from itself," and, most famous of all in the age of Trump, "Everyone is entitled to his own opinion but not his own facts." As Moynihan quickly discovered, government is not necessarily the best place to practice your wit, and certainly not at the time he served in it. He was, however, the only one of the thinkers I am discussing who did so serve—one reason he is still missed by so many (including me).

Irony will always serve as an alternative to those tempted to allow their minds to be captured by theory, ideology, or principle. This is important to remember, since irony has gone so much out of fashion in recent decades. Our public life has simply become too literal for its own good. Today's right-wing conservatives, unlike past figures such as H. L. Mencken, Albert Jay Nock, and William Buckley Jr., have no sense of irony at all; they write as if the world is coming to an end save for their efforts to wake us up to the actions of treasonous Democrats. Alas, on this point left-wing writers seem to meet them on their own terms, writing in as serious a tone as they can convey. (The exception is the subversive tone adopted by today's comedians, a topic I will address in the next chapter.) Both sides bite off their words. Both sides are guilty of excessive sarcasm. Both sides feature ponderous writing. Political debate in America today resembles a spelling bee in which youngsters concentrate with superhuman intensity to get the right answer. No wonder that political campaigns, as important as they are in choosing our leaders, are such dreadful experiences to watch. One longs for just a touch of skepticism, the kind of move that came so naturally to John F. Kennedy or Barack Obama (but not, alas, Hillary Clinton). Obama, indeed, was a walking tangle of ironies: a black man who was half-white and urged us to transcend race; a centrist who could not find centrists on the other side to meet him halfway; a Christian realist inspired by hope.[34] If our politics could somehow lighten up, energy and enthusiasm would burst out.

In 1956, President and Mrs. Eisenhower invited every single senator to a party at the White House, with one conspicuous exception. Joe McCarthy had lost his power to investigate when the Democrats regained control of Congress in 1954. His health had declined as rapidly as his influence. Shunned, lonely, bitter, and betrayed, McCarthy suffered a severe fall for a man who had once terrorized much of the country. And there was a great irony at work: although McCarthy was as free as ever to peddle conspiracy theories, there existed something of a real conspiracy among those journalists and editors who consciously decided no longer to pay much attention to him. He died on May 2, 1957.

McCarthy damaged numerous individual lives. But the greater damage he caused was to America's way of conducting politics. We know this because our current president is so much like him. Donald Trump is an incorrigible liar and well-practiced demagogue. When he first considered a run for the presidency, his political views were something of a blank slate, but he eventually campaigned, and has been governing, from the same side of the political spectrum as his inquisitorial predecessor. Both men displayed a taste for conspiracy theorizing. Insinuation was for each the preferred method of domination. They even relied upon the same person, the notorious fixer Roy Cohn, to keep them out of trouble. Although the mass media changed dramatically from the one era to the other—McCarthy with a Twitter account? The mind reels—both used what was available to them in equally supercharged ways. It is true that they had different views of Russia, the earlier one con and the later other pro, but even there McCarthy's focus was more on alleged domestic subversion and, like Trump, not on the conduct of Russian foreign policy. Only on the question of alcohol did their lives and habits truly diverge: Trump is a teetotaler, while McCarthy drank himself into personal and political oblivion.

I wish it were true, as Karl Marx once wrote, that history repeats itself, the second time as farce. There is nothing farcical about Donald Trump. Those who ask how Americans could have chosen this man as president ought to ask first how the good people of Wisconsin could have chosen Joe McCarthy as their senator. America's willingness to elect demagogues to important positions in public life goes on and on. Fortunately the earlier one's conspiracy theorizing and bad temper came to an end relatively soon after he began. There is no way of knowing when the career of the current one will come to its conclusion. It would be the height of irony, and therefore something to hope for, if Donald Trump, and all the suspicion he has imposed on American public life, were to aid in the process of doing him in.

5
TRAGEDY, COMEDY, AND AMERICAN DEMOCRACY

Trump Presents—the play that opened in Washington after the 2016 election—has an indefinite closure date: it may run for four years, eight years, or close sooner than advertised. For an audience seeking either the high drama of tragedy or the belly-laugh relief of comedy, however, this theatrical entertainment has little or nothing to offer: do not expect to find in America's currently running political drama anything as noble as the prince of Denmark or as witty as Rosalind in *As You Like It*. "Humor," Reinhold Niebuhr declared, "is a prelude to faith": we laugh at the everyday incongruities we experience only to prepare us for the cosmic incongruities of our existence, an attitude that ought to be as important for secular people as for religious ones.[1] Meanwhile tragedy defines our very condition as modern people; for Niebuhr nothing was more tragic than our need to make nuclear weapons in order to prevent their use.[2] As Niebuhr's thoughts suggest, neither denying that tragic choices must be made nor ridding ourselves of an appreciation of the absurd can be of much help in making sense of our collective lives.

Democracy needs tragedy, even if democratic citizens find tragedy awful to experience. The promise of modern democracy is the idea that ultimately the people will get what they want. But no diverse and pluralistic society can give everyone everything they want. The art of governing in a democracy, therefore, is either to choose among alternatives or to find compromises between them. If there are going to be winners, there will have to be losers. It is no occasion for triumph if the winners feel good about their situation; the real challenge in democracy lies in explaining to the losers why they should never give up. This applies as much to those who disdain Trump even though he was duly elected as it does to those who wished to see Obamacare repealed even though it has (so far) survived.

Conservatism has in the past offered a method of explaining to losers why their losses are justified: no one ever said our world was perfect, and some people are simply born unlucky; of a disadvantaged race, class, or gender; without the necessary talents; or lacking in self-control. The problem today is that conservatives have no such tragic inclinations in their arsenal. In its response to decisions that bring succor to some and pain to others, as we can see in contemporary debates over health care, tax policy, or immigration, the conservative instinct is to deny that any such tragic choices are necessary. Conservatism, at least as embodied in the contemporary Republican Party so strongly living in the shadow of Ronald Reagan, has been all about promising the wonders to be achieved with no mention of the costs to be paid.

Democracy demands comedy as well. If tragedy historically led us never to find hope, comedy in the past chipped in to protect us against hoping too much. Comedy's greatest task is to remind us that politics, like life, has its moments of absurdity and ineffability. Comedy is essential for liberal democracy because the fundamental inclination of liberals is to plan, but, as the conservative is always there to remind us, the future, as we know from the sociological discussion of unanticipated consequences, can never be perfectly anticipated. In planning for efficiency in a not-always perfect world, liberals ought to recognize that God, as Niebuhr told us, is laughing at us and especially at our pretensions. (If not God, then fate, luck, or irony.) Liberalism can, if it wishes, be ambitious, but it must also teach uncertainty, modesty, and irony. Yet liberals in contemporary America have become frozen in fixed faces of disapproval, opposed to what conservatives want but no longer certain what they do. If rightists have become liberals in their utopianism, leftists, who appreciate all the gains they have made and now worry that they will be taken away, have become reactionary in their negativity.

Comedy, which became a liberal virtue in the years after which the mature liberals wrote, is now as difficult to find on the left as tragedy is on the right. As important as a comic perspective may be for soothing hurts, and in that way helping democracy survive, our intense controversies over political correctness demonstrate that leftists have become too serious for their own good. Distinctions between individuals, rather than being celebrated because variety makes the world more interesting, are, out of the strictest possible definition of equality, all too often perceived as an invidious force dividing in order to conquer. Leftists are far too fearful of giving offense to offer humor. Opposed to censorship by the government, they censor each other with the zeal of Puritan divines. Leftists take politics with such a fearful seriousness that one constantly fears that if they fail at the give-and-take that democracy requires, their world will come crashing down. Fragility in the face of the absurd cannot possibly serve liberal ends. Liberals appear brittle and ineffective because, unable to laugh at much of anything, they take every political struggle in which they are involved as a do-or-die affair. With the stakes that high, who can afford humor?

Either the conservative loss of the tragic or the liberal displacement of the comic by itself would create problems enough for our political system. But when both join together as they have in recent years, the effect is a double whammy, exposing our informal norms for how our politics should work to pressures from opposite directions at the same time. A people that does not know whether to laugh or cry is in serious political trouble. Our situation will not be improved until American politics once again values even a smattering of the emotions that make for great theater. At the present moment, that seems even more difficult to achieve than bringing populism under control, overcoming the effects of mass society, or reducing the negative consequences of conspiracy theorizing.

Because they wrote in such trying times, one might expect a tone of gloom among the mature liberals. To some extent this is true: the public intellectuals who were born in Europe, as well as those who studied that continent, could not help but see Hannah Arendt's "dark times" everywhere they turned. But here, as in so many other ways, American thinkers added their own twist. If there is one defining feature of American culture, in the view of Niebuhr, Lionel Trilling, and the other mature liberals, it is the absence of anything resembling a Shakespearean view of the world, tragic or comic. We lack seriousness in the way we think, and the result is an immature simple-mindedness in our politics that corresponds to the moral superficiality of our literature. Our literary world, Dwight Macdonald wrote in this vein, is "flat," and only such flatness can explain the popularity of writers so lacking in talent as Norman Cousins or, no relation, James Gould Cozzens.[3]

Our flatness, as it happens, has the same cause as the lowering of the level of our political discourse: populism. Our imaginative writers struggle (and fail) to deal with what Trilling called "the American populist feeling against mind, against the expert, the theorists, and the brain-truster."[4] Trilling was not one of those thinkers who declared that everything that had happened on the scene before him had become cheap and tawdry; in fact, "there is an unmistakable improvement in the American cultural situation of today over that of, say, thirty years ago."[5] But a certain American wish to escape from complexity was for him an unavoidable by-product of how we think. "Our liberal ideology," as he put it, "has produced a large literature of social and political protest, but not, for several decades, a single writer who commands our real literary admiration; we all respond to the flattery of agreement but perhaps even the simplest reader among us knows in his heart the difference between that emotion and the real emotions of literature. . . . Our dominant literature is profitable in the degree that it is earnest, sincere, and solemn. . . . It has neither imagination nor mind."[6] If too immature a liberalism can do that to literature, it is frightening to contemplate what it can do to politics.

Given the horrors of the years in which they lived, the mature liberals paid far more attention to the tragic than to the comic. But as writers interested in all of the peculiarities of the human condition, they never neglected the comic dimensions of life. Consider again

Trilling, a serious man if there ever was one. Trilling did not consider Mark Twain a comic writer; instead he viewed *Huckleberry Finn* as a subversive book: "No one who reads thoughtfully the dialectic of Huck's great moral crisis will ever again be wholly able to accept with some question and some irony the assumptions of the respectable morality by which he lives, nor will ever again be certain that what he considers the clear dictates of moral reason are not merely the engrained customary beliefs of this time and place."[7]

Fortunately, however, in the years after World War II there appeared a new comic voice in American literature: Saul Bellow's. In his review of *The Adventures of Augie March*, Trilling compared Bellow favorably to the left-wing writers influenced by the Communist Party, who stripped the humanness from their characters to deliver without much nuance one social morality play after another. Bellow, by contrast, was willing to take a comic perspective on the grim urban realities that other writers could only denounce, and in that way gave his characters the gift of dignity. In this lies the virtue of the comic: we are reminded that "whatever fixes life and specializes and limits a person to a function, whether it be that of a social class, a theory, or a principle, endangers the wholeness of the self which makes possible the relation to and the perception of one's fellow men."[8] Trilling was an early critic of political correctness. In fact, the term was first used in the 1930s to describe those who held to whatever the position of the Communist Party on the issue of the day happened to be, as did the socialist realist writers for whom Trilling had such contempt. If the implication was not clear, it should have been: a text without humor is a text likely to be preferred by authoritarians.

Even when the mature liberals were not addressing the question of comedy per se, their writing style could venture past the ironic and into the comic. The humor that appears in the books and essays of Richard Hofstadter and Daniel Patrick Moynihan, to name two, is clearly meant to warn us against taking ourselves too seriously. A well-crafted use of the comic also characterized the writing of Peter Viereck, the one conservative asked to contribute to *The New American Right*. A writer of quite exuberant prose, Viereck is remembered, if at all, for saying that "Catholic-baiting is the anti-Semitism of the liberals" and for his use of the term, later adopted and transformed into an ugly one by Rush Limbaugh, "comminazis."[9] His pen was wicked. Richard Nixon, to take just one example, was "an Arrow color ad . . . eager eyed, clean-shaven, and grinning boyishly while he assesses the precise spot for the stiletto."[10] (Ironically Nixon may have lost his presidential campaign five years after these words appeared because he did not appear to be clean-shaven.) Viereck was included in the Bell book because, as an old-fashioned conservative traditionalist, he was a severe critic of the populistic masses who seemed to love McCarthy. But Viereck never became a conservative in good standing; the right's anti-intellectualism in the 1940s and 1950s shifted easily into distaste for writers having fun with their prose.

The mature liberals wrote out of a fear that the full range of emotions experienced through the reading and watching of great works of art was in the process of disappearing. What was then a fear has, in the age of Trump, become a reality. The story of how this happened is one of the most important of all our stories because it has so shaped the palpable sense that we no longer know what we stand for as a people. We strike out in blind rage against those who pose no threat to us or we treat them with unnecessary contempt because, deprived of both comedy and tragedy, we have no way of knowing the plot of the play we are in. An astounding 80 percent of Americans believe that the people running the country do not care about them, and 68 percent report that what they think does not count for much anymore.[11] No wonder Americans are so politically alienated. As a spectacle, their political system has little to offer them.

Before liberalism developed in the late eighteenth century, conservatives found the reason for tragedy in God or nature or both. Some force larger than ourselves created the world around us, and if that world is unjust or unfair, this is only what the creator decided was best, and often for reasons unintelligible to the rest of us. It would be just as absurd to tell a monarch that you disagree with his decision to go to war as it would be to tell God that his flood, hurricane, or drought came at precisely the wrong moment. We cannot escape the arbitrary rule of tyrants for the same reason that Oedipus slept with his mother: destiny rules us. Even a nontheistic writer such as Thomas Hobbes, who was not a conservative but who shared a conservative taste for order, was certain of our inability to govern ourselves; for him it was not so much nature as human nature that causes us to require authority. What can one expect when life is solitary, poor, nasty, brutish, and short, other than gratitude for the last of these?

In Europe, conservatism made a certain amount of sense because there was so much to conserve: the monarchy, the church, and the nobility stood for, even if at times badly, stability, order, and tradition. The defense of those institutions could take many forms, but Edmund Burke offered an account of them that has had lasting appeal: we should conserve these institutions because together they embody magnificence. If it takes a very long sentence to convey what he meant, it is worth it for the splendor of his prose:

> Indeed, when I consider the face of the kingdom of France, the multitude and opulence of her cities, the useful magnificence of her spacious high roads and bridges, the opportunity of her artificial canals and navigations opening the conveniences of maritime communication through a solid continent of so immense an extent; when I turn my eyes to the stupendous works of her ports and harbors, and to her whole naval apparatus, whether for war or trade; when I bring before my view the number of her fortifications, constructed with so bold and masterly a skill and made and maintained at so prodigious a charge, presenting an armed front and impenetrable barrier to her enemies upon every side; when I recollect how very small a part of that extensive region is without cultivation, and to what complete perfection the culture of many of the best productions of the earth have been brought in France; when I reflect on the excellence of her manufactures and fabrics, second to none but ours, and in some particulars not second; when I contemplate the grand foundations of charity, public and private; when I survey

> the state of all the arts that beautify and polish life; when I reckon the men she has bred for extending her fame in war, her able statesmen, the multitude of her profound lawyers and theologians, her philosophers, her critics, her historians and antiquaries, her poets and her orators, sacred and profane—I behold in all this something which awes and commands the imagination, which checks the mind on the brink of precipitate and indiscriminate censure, and which demands that we should very seriously examine what and how great are the latent vices that could authorize us at once to level so spacious a fabric with the ground.[12]

Why, then, should losers accept the decisions of the winners? Primarily, Burke argued, for aesthetic reasons: what a tragedy it would be if, because of the mistaken egoism of all those inferior people intent on satisfying their own selfish needs, this entire beautiful edifice came crashing down. What liberals universally applaud—expanded suffrage and a greater voice for the people—Burke viewed as insufferable.

While impassioned, Burke's conservatism was less than pure: obedience, in his view, has reasons behind it, such as preserving glory, making it anything but arbitrary. Burke thus left the field open for more radically conservative thinkers to make the case that even if the monarchy or nobility fail at doing anything positive, even if their legacy is nothing short of pure evil, and even if their commands are simply whimsical, they still must be obeyed. The thinker who best made this case was, like the Irishman Burke, an opponent of the French Revolution who also belonged to a national minority group: the Savoyard Joseph de Maistre.

As a traditional European conservative, Maistre believed that the church and the monarchy constituted the origin and essence of sovereignty. What made Maistre distinctive, however, is that no attempt at pleasing metaphors or forgiving excuses mars the brutal truth that when it comes to politics, authority is everything: "The sword of justice," as he brilliantly put it, "has no sheath." Maistre's prose could be as splendid as Burke's; man, he wrote, "kills to nourish himself, he kills to clothe himself, he kills to adorn himself, he kills to attack, he kills to defend himself, he kills to instruct himself, he kills to amuse himself, he kills to kill." His representative on earth, as difficult as the idea may be to accept, is therefore the executioner, the one last person standing between the sinner and the punishment justifiably waiting for him. The man who chooses this position may seem like the rest of us, "but he is an extraordinary being, and for him to be brought into existence as a member of the human family, a decree was required, a FIAT of creative power. He is created as a law on to himself."[13] Strip Burke's magnificence down to its essence, and you are left with the executioner. It is as if democracy permanently wears a black hood covering its face.

No such conservative writing could ever be taken seriously in the United States. One of the most insightful of the mature liberals—Louis Hartz—explained why. If we take Maistre or Burke as the primary sources for conservatism, no American thinker has ever gone as far as these Europeans, he argued, in justifying authority. The closest we ever came was in the pre–Civil War South, yet even that society's greatest defenders, such as John C. Calhoun, could never speak in European tones. Calhoun sought to tinker with our political arrangements, not to speculate on the nature of God or the power of history. Like those of any other country, America's leaders required sovereignty. But unlike all other countries, it lacked forceful arguments on sovereignty's behalf. As Hartz wrote of the efforts by southerners to justify their way of life, "When one piles these contradictions on top of the others, one gets an almost frightening sense of how hard it was to be a reactionary in the South."[14] Once political power is no longer justified by monarchical or religious authority, in short, the only place left to turn is to liberal political theory, and under liberal political theory slavery was ultimately doomed.

If there existed any rival to the South for championing ostensibly nonliberal ideas, it came from the powerful titans of industry who appeared in the northern states during the Gilded Age. Yet here as well, Hartz argued, liberalism reared its unwanted head in unexpected ways. One spirit, and one spirit alone, dominated American thought between Appomattox and the Great Depression, Hartz believed: that of Horatio Alger. The highly individualistic notion that through hard work and diligence anyone could fight their way to the top undermined both revolutionary socialism and pure Social Darwinist capitalism. Workers in America believed that they owned their own labor—so much for Marx. And capitalists discovered that, just as Alger's hero received help on his way up, they could help themselves by coming together in huge trusts—so much for Herbert Spencer, the English Social Darwinist. When capitalist imperatives and labor's hope for improvement merged together in the form of the New Deal, the result was the tempering of the expectations of both. There was no room in this compromise for the Marxist radical, but neither was there room for the European successors of Burke and Maistre.

Nothing significant has changed in the nature of American conservatism since Hartz published his book. Conservatism and the Republican Party took such political hits during the Great Depression and World War II that Franklin Delano Roosevelt was elected four times as president. Even when conservatism began to stir again, in the postwar years that brought us Joseph McCarthy, it did so in decidedly non-European form. In European terms, as I suggested earlier, McCarthy was a populist, not a conservative. His crusade was too working class, too Irish, and too midwestern for a typical European conservative to sign on.

There did exist one possibility for a revived American conservatism in the years after World War II, but its fate suggested why such a genuine conservatism was so difficult to fashion in this country. The right-wing European intellectuals who moved to this country during periods of great turmoil in their home countries all faced the same dilemma: adapt to America and flourish or maintain one's ideas and be shuttled to the sidelines. Leo Strauss, for example, who found more wisdom in the ancients than in the moderns, inspired a number of followers who saw in American leaders such as Abraham Lincoln examples of homegrown political genius. The members of the Austrian school of economics, defenders of laissez-faire in all things, modified few or none of their ideas after coming to America, but they remained academic theorists more than governmental advisers. Traditional

European Catholic conservatives were at a loss to deal with American Catholic workers firmly committed to the New Deal and influential in the Democratic Party because they were not attracted to isolationism, particularly when it came to such countries as Poland or Hungary. The one homegrown thinker said to be the American version of Edmund Burke, Russell Kirk, was a rather shallow one, precisely because, as Hartz taught us, American conservatives lack the traditions and history of a true conservative consciousness. Agrarians, finally, in an increasingly urban society, had little to offer people outside the South.

The result was that American conservatism became a complete mess. Traditionalists clashed with free-marketers. Isolationists and interventionists rarely saw eye to eye. European Protestants and Catholics, and especially the latter, brought their theological disputes to this country. Hartz had found little role for genuine conservatism in eighteenth- and nineteenth-century America. The twentieth needed to see something new if conservatism were to be a force in American life, and nothing along those lines appeared.

The outstanding historian of American conservative thought, George H. Nash, fully aware of the many contradictions between all the American conservatisms, suggested one possible solution: borrowing from the former Marxist firebrand Frank Meyer, he called the postwar synthesis "fusionism," a blending of agrarians, libertarians, traditionalists, and anti-Communists in a common critique of America's direction.[15] Fusionism did not solve the tension within the right so much as displace it to the future. It was also the right's version of opportunism: let's downplay our differences in order to solidify our strengths.

Fusionism did work for a while, but the price paid for its new unanimity was high: there turned out to be only one current of thought on which all the different strands of conservatives could agree, and that was hatred of liberalism. In an irony earlier conservatives would have understood, fusionism thereby tied conservatism's fate to the future of liberalism. When liberalism was strong, as during the New Deal, conservatism was weak. But as liberalism began to lose its appeal, conservatism began to attract votes. And so it happened: the very radical right the mature liberals feared so much in the 1950s finally come to power with the Reagan victory in 1980.

Reaganism, it turned out, was a mixed blessing for conservatism. Many previously unemployed conservatives found jobs in the new administration, and large numbers of American voters loved and still love the man. But with Reagan it became clear to all that the price of power for American conservatism was the relinquishment of anything resembling the tragic. Reagan was a near-perfect exemplar of typical American optimism, and he based his popularity on the sunniest vision of America's promise he could find. The American thinker who came closest to understanding this was the historian John Patrick Diggins, who found in Reagan something closer to Tom Paine than to Edmund Burke, let alone Joseph de Maistre.[16] The journey from a strict Calvinism that sought severe punishment for all sins to a Republican president certain of America's inherent goodness in the world was more than a huge step. It was the toppling of a deeply religious point of view into the program of a political party bent upon holding political power as firmly as possible no matter what it took to get them there. Reagan created Reaganism, but he did very little to help American conservatism find an authentic voice.

Fusionism is interesting for another significant irony: the thinker who was most useful in providing the glue that unified conservatives was a liberal: once again, Lionel Trilling. In perhaps his most cited work, and certainly one of the shortest, the preface he wrote to his book *Beyond Culture* (1965), Trilling viewed the emerging New Left as an embodiment of what he called the "adversary culture," those intellectuals and activists who opposed the dominant American culture, expressing their discontent through either left-wing politics or the discovery of the ecstatic. The phrase quickly caught on. A leading neoconservative, Norman Podhoretz, a student of Trilling's, was fond of using it, as was Irving Kristol; the concept of the adversary culture, in fact, become the singular statement of what we now call neoconservatism. The concept also led the more intellectually oriented American conservatives, in the past followers of Leon Trotsky, to a right-wing version of the class struggle. Following Trilling, who had suggested that "around the adversary culture there has formed what I call a class . . . that is not without power, and . . . we can say . . . that it seeks to aggrandize and perpetuate itself," liberals, intellectuals, and public-policy bureaucrats were portrayed as a "new class" taking advantage of their abilities as writers and thinkers to fashion a society in their own image—and for their own benefit.[17]

The effects of all of these changes in conservative doctrine can be seen in the stands taken by the Republican Party today: its self-congratulation, its flirtations with populism, and its unstoppable overpromising. Supply-side economics offers the most obvious example. Although pretty much all of contemporary history proves the opposite, today's Republicans tell us that we can balance the budget (a good thing) while cutting taxes (also a good thing.) Even though such a policy has never worked, the Trump administration, like every other recent Republican administration, used the failed rationale of supply-side economics to justify its wildly irresponsible and perniciously unfair tax cuts of December 2017. Nor are taxes the only example of right-wing tragedy-avoidance. For seven long years, conservatives promised, without a shred of realism, that they could supply universal health insurance with fewer restrictions than Obamacare, itself a product of a more realistic conservatism. That utopian thinking was smashed after Republicans finally won control of all the branches of government, only to realize that the world was more complicated than they had ever let on to their followers—or, in some cases, to themselves. They also promised those followers that it would be easy to control immigration—a little more strict law enforcement should do the trick—which turned out to be as illusory as their promises on health care. By 2018, the Republican Party had left the tragic so far behind that few could believe it had recently shared a worldview committed to explaining why fate or the divine or history made it impossible to obtain most of what we want.

The Greeks, who fully understood the importance of tragedy, would have recognized the Republican imbroglio; they called it hubris. By cutting their ties with tragedy, Republicans were left adrift. They desperately wanted to tell Americans many things. Americans have it too good. They cannot continue to demand benefits without facing the inflationary consequences later. The slothful among the masses of people deserve their fate, and God frowns on their profligacy. America cannot intervene everywhere around the world whenever a crisis arises. It must carefully manage its resources. Global warming is not wreaking havoc with the weather. Not all diseases have a cure. America needs to offer special privileges to the wealthy and the powerful because, being wealthy and powerful, they deserve them. Puerto Ricans are not "real" Americans, and no attention needs to be paid to their humanitarian disaster. Too much attention has been paid to the blacks, and it is now time to reward the whites. Tanks and military gear will make America's streets safe at long last. A newly built wall will stop the flow of foreigners to America. But none of these promises could ever be fulfilled. The tragic had become the fantastic. Republican conservatives did not know what had hit them.

All may not be lost for conservatives, however. We will be able to mark the moment when the Republicans finally come to realize how far they have left the tragic behind. It will take a senator such as Ted Cruz of Texas, who voted against hurricane assistance when Katrina devastated New Orleans, to tell his own voters that consistency in conservative principle demands that there will be no aid for them in the wake of a hurricane there. Or conservative Republicans in the House could announce that the whole point of their party's efforts at "tax reform" is to lower the burden on the rich because, frankly, they deserve it, and in that spirit leave few or none of the deductions relied upon by the middle class. Should anyone say that it would be wildly unrealistic for conservatives to be forthright about their intentions because democracy demands that we give the people what they want, we have the voice of Edmund Burke to rely upon. In his speech to the electors of Bristol, he famously declared: "Your representative owes you not his industry only, but his judgment; and he betrays, instead of serving you, if he sacrifices it to your opinion."[18] All too many conservatives today not only betray the ideas of their past greats; they betray as well their advice for holding office. In contemporary America, where acceptance of tragedy is a thing of the past, the rush of conservatives never to exercise judgment is striking.

As is the case with so many other features of American politics, we owe our fascination with comedy, and especially those forms of comedy that poke fun at rulers, to the ancient Greeks. Aristophanes, often called the father of comedy, was especially important in this regard. We have already seen how the American framers, worried about the potential impact of demagogues, considered Cleon of Athens exactly the kind of leader to be avoided. Aristophanes helped shape Cleon's negative reputation.[19] When under attack by rebels in the *Knights*, Cleon pleads for help, but the leader of the chorus offers no sympathy:

> You devour the public funds that all should share in; you treat the treasury officials like the fruit of the fig tree, squeezing them to find which are still green or more or less ripe; and, when you find a simple and timid one, you force him to come back from the Chersonese [today the southeastern Balkans], then you seize him by the middle, throttle him by the neck, while you twist his shoulder back; he falls and you devour him. Besides, you know very well how to select from among the citizens those who are as meek as lambs, rich, without guile and loathers or lawsuits.[20]

Thus was a dialectic established that has lasted until the present: even if not much can be done to rein in tyrants through directly political means, comedy is always there as a safety valve.

Conservatives such as Burke and Maistre knew what to revere. Yet the very institutions that they viewed as guardians of the ancient regime were the same institutions that masters of comedy loved to attack: the church, the monarchy, and the nobility. Following in the footsteps of the Roman poet Juvenal, artists in Europe, such as Giovanni Boccaccio, William Hogarth, Geoffrey Chaucer, Voltaire, and Molière, drew laughs from their portraits of lustful or hypocritical aristocrats. But it was the First Estate, the church, which received the greatest amount of mockery. Even among believers themselves, not everything religious was treated as sanctified: Martin Luther, the Don Rickles of the Protestant Reformation, was a master of one-line putdowns, as in "The Franciscans are the lice which the devil put into the fur-coat of God" or "When I fart in Wittenberg, the Pope in Rome wrinkles his nose."[21] It cannot be a complete surprise that one of the leading religious sociologists of our era, Peter Berger, wrote a book about laughter or that one of our leading satirists, Stephen Colbert, talks so much about his Catholic faith.[22] It is odd but true that one of the things we have inherited from the age of faith is the capacity to make fun of faith.

If conservatives in the past possessed an elective affinity with tragedy, the same is not true with respect to liberals and comedy: before the rise of liberal democracy, the main form that comedy took was satire, and satire, although oppositional, belonged to no particular class or ideology. The work often cited as the greatest satire in the English language, *A Modest Proposal*, for example, was written by Jonathan Swift, a Tory in his political views and a defender of the Church of Ireland in his religious ones. Swift's friends among the satiric writers of his generation, such as Joseph Addison and Richard Steele, were Whigs, but of the most respectful sort. Together with John Gay and Alexander Pope, Swift was an active member of the Scriblerus Club, devoted to attacking obscure and impenetrable learned writing, the sort of thing academics up for tenure today are expected to produce, but without the satire.

One particularly fascinating example of nineteenth-century political satire was written by the French publicist Maurice Joly (1829–1878), a royalist and reactionary. Joly's major work was his *Dialogue in Hell between Machiavelli and Montesquieu* (1864) under a pseudonym. Both men were condemned to hell, in Joly's account, because one, Montesquieu, had helped bring liberalism into being and because the other, Machiavelli, challenged unquestioning absolutism. The dialogue makes for fascinating reading, even today, because Machiavelli argued that a return to absolutism awaits us "within a century," while

Montesquieu points to the new democracy being formed across the Atlantic as the harbinger of the future: "You have spoken to me of the United States of America: I do not know if you are a new Washington, but it is certain that the current constitution of the United States was discussed, deliberated and voted upon by the nation's representatives."[23] Joly was arrested and imprisoned after his authorship was discovered, his book was banned, and he eventually committed suicide. He might well have been completely forgotten except for the fact, which itself sounds like the plot of a satiric pamphlet, that the book was later plagiarized by the writers of the notoriously anti-Semitic *The Protocols of the Elders of Zion*.

If satire in Europe tended to be multidirectional in its politics, the same was not true in the United States. America lacked a state church, a monarchy, and an entrenched nobility to satirize, and the conservatism of the Scriblerus Club did not have an audience. What was left to mock? The great student of American life, Alexis de Tocqueville, answered by suggesting that we were simply not a very funny people. It is true that Americans were "placed in the happiest circumstances that the world affords," yet "it seemed to me as if a cloud habitually hung upon their brow, and I thought them serious and sad even in their pleasures." The trouble, as always, was democracy. American democracy during Tocqueville's visit was, in today's metaphor, a rat race: without secure positions, the temptation to rise higher became more common, paradoxically making it more difficult for anyone to actually do so. "In democratic times enjoyments are more intense than in the ages of aristocracy, and the number of those who partake in them is vastly larger, but, on the other hand, it must be admitted that man's hopes and desires are often blasted, the soul is more stricken, and care itself more keen."[24]

This dour atmosphere naturally influenced how Americans experience the arts. Arriving in the United States from a country renowned for its playwrights, Tocqueville understood that theater is among the most democratic of the arts, for literacy is not required of its audience, no advanced study is necessary, and the emotions of the heart are valued more than the syllogisms of the head. For all this, however, the American theater was incapable of producing a Racine, so alien were Americans to the traditions established by classical writers. Great comedy was as rare as great tragedy. Satire makes fun of the powerful, but in a democracy the people are the ultimate power—who would pay good money to see themselves made fun of on the stage? In France, Molière satirized a well-off son of a cloth merchant, M. Jourdain, the *bourgeois gentilhomme* who tried to ape the aristocracy. In America, if we extend Tocqueville's thoughts, everyone would have a touch of M. Jourdain about him.

Had Tocqueville visited after the Civil War, no doubt he would have noted that the political cartoon was even easier to grasp than an evening at the theater. These were the years in which the most important comic pen in America belonged to the cartoonist Thomas Nast. Nast had numerous enemies, and he attacked them all vehemently.[25] Although born Catholic, he hated Catholicism and in particular its political allies, such as the Democratic Party and New York City's Tammany Hall. He was a Republican through and through and worked tirelessly on behalf of Abraham Lincoln. His greatest cartoons, many believe, appeared in 1871 and 1872 and helped Ulysses S. Grant win his second term as president. In my opinion, however, his most trenchant cartoon, and the one with the greatest relevance for our time, is "Compromise with the South (1864)," in which a humiliated Union soldier shakes hands with Robert E. Lee over the grave of another Union soldier with Columbia ("The gem of the ocean") crying in her hands. It is as if Nast knew, before the Civil War even ended, that eventually the Union troops would have died in vain, for the South did rise again, politically, and at no time more noteworthily and notoriously than at the present.

Nast is important for another reason: he was an immigrant, from Bavaria. In Europe, comedy and satire were traditionally directed against the foibles of bumbling or hypocritical aristocrats or learned professionals. But in this country, where class conflict was so muted, comedy became the means by which new immigrants could take some of the pain out of their often-difficult accommodation to American life. The great wave of immigration at the end of the nineteenth century

and the beginning of the twentieth brought to these shores an astonishing number of very funny people. They settled in the cities, where nightclubs, dance halls, and eventually speakeasies became plentiful. Forced to learn (and perform) in a new language, unless they were Irish or Jews appearing in the Yiddish theater, they acquired considerable verbal agility. Financed by fellow ethnics, including those who specialized in criminal enterprise, they themselves were not always rule-abiding good citizens. They and their children would flourish on radio, and some eventually made it as well on television. They brought a distinct style of comic humor to America: biting, lasting, and above all else, political. African Americans also took part in this comic revival; one of Eddie Cantor's costars was Bert Williams, "considered by some historians," as Kliph Nesteroff put it, "as the greatest African-American comedian who ever lived."[26]

The ethnic group whose humor made the biggest impact on American life, at least by the number of stars it produced, was the Jews: besides Eddie Cantor, there was Jack Benny, Sid Caesar, Milton Berle, George Jessel, the Three Stooges, Danny Kaye, George Burns, Jerry Lewis, Ed Wynn, Rodney Dangerfield, Victor Borge, Judy Holliday,

Phil Silvers, and, eventually, Mel Brooks, Carl Reiner, Madeline Kahn, Joan Rivers, Phyllis Diller, Jerry Seinfeld, Jon Stewart, Bette Midler, Larry David, Gilda Radner, Louis C. K., Sarah Silverman, and numerous others. I cite the Jews rather than, say, the Irish or the Italians, not out of ethnic pride, even if the country from which my maternal grandparents emigrated, Hungary, once had a lively tradition of Jewish comedy.[27] The Jewish example is important for another reason. While all ethnic groups can relate their share of tragedy—the Irish potato famine and the Armenian genocide, for example—anti-Semitism, leading up to the Holocaust, was an especially unfunny matter. That the Jews managed to laugh, even poking fun at Hitler in Mel Brooks's blasphemous *The Producers*, was testimony to the power of comedy.

Of all the Jewish comics who came to America, the most influential were the Marx Brothers. Here was ethnic humor run rampant. In *A Night at the Opera* (1935), Groucho plays Otis B. Driftwood, whose antics take place in front of the most upper-class form of musical and dramatic entertainment. Also satirized is the WASP Mrs. Claypool, played by Margaret Dumont, who, as nearly always in the Marx Brothers' films, is the target of Groucho's many escapades but provides the money for whatever is taking place in the background. Immigration itself, furthermore, makes its way into the film as two of the brothers, plus another character, sneak into the country disguised as famous aviators. The sheer manic energy of the Marx Brothers, the constant shifts of character they undergo, their making fun of who and what they meet along the way, the puns—all hint at a clash between the Old World and the New. "Restrict immigration," Groucho suggests after Chico mistakes "mutinies" for "matinees" in *Monkey Business*. They would make fun of anything, even what had brought their parents to this country.

When asked about politics, Groucho Marx denied any particular point of view, saying, "We were just four Jews trying to get a laugh."[28] But the targets of the brothers suggest otherwise. Indeed, *Duck Soup* (1933) dealt directly with the dictators then coming to power in Italy and Germany. In no other Marx Brothers film were the targets, tinhorn dictators, so clear. Mussolini knew this and had the film banned in Italy. Now that America has a president who shares the authoritarianism of the twentieth century's leading demagogues, it will be interesting to see if his term is accompanied by a Marx Brothers revival. At least one writer has already made the connection. "Both dismiss the advice of establishment figures," Luke Epplin writes of Groucho Marx (as Rufus T. Firefly in *Duck Soup*) and Donald Trump, and "are too distracted with personal grievances to delve into policy details, and have checkered histories of reneging on promised payments. Even their physical characteristics bear some resemblance, with Trump's preposterous hairdo standing in for Groucho's equally preposterous greasepaint mustache. They wear their deceptions right on their faces."[29]

After the Marx Brothers, political comedy began to take its rightful ideological place in America on the left side of the political fence. Interestingly enough, the political event that did so much to stimulate the reflections of the mature liberals also helped animate American comedy and its spirit of political opposition: the witch hunt led by Joe McCarthy. Publicity hungry, McCarthy targeted Hollywood, which was where, along with New York, American comedians perfected their art. Some in the comic world, such as Lou Costello, were enthusiastic backers of McCarthy, but in general the entertainment community saw the blacklist as a huge threat to the integrity of artistic expression. Whether it was McCarthy himself or the general malaise that seemed to characterize the Eisenhower years, American comedy experienced its greatest breakthrough during the years of the McCarthy inquisition, as Mort Sahl, Lenny Bruce, Jonathan Winters, Tom Lehrer, Dick Gregory, Shelley Berman, Mike Nichols and Elaine May, and even Woody Allen, who started out as a screenwriter, all began their careers. There was no mistaking the point of view that these comics took: whatever their race, ethnicity, or gender, all of them were critics of what was happening in their country.

It was during these years that liberalism and comedy came together in what seemed an unshakable alliance. Conservatism was patriotic, conformist, and, to the degree that it laughed, amused by Bob Hope and Martha Raye. The left was urban, disrespectful, scatological, pleasure seeking, ethnic, and uproarious. An entire generation grew up thinking that left-wing politics was the stuff not only of marches on Washington but of Greenwich Village, the drug culture, and hippies. Abbie Hoffman and Jerry Rubin embodied this absurdist side of the New Left, dropping dollar bills from the gallery of the New York Stock Exchange or appearing in Revolutionary War getup before the House Un-American Activities Committee. Paul Krassner published *The Realist*, a magazine of political satire that had more in common with *Mad Magazine* than with Jonathan Swift. Barbara Garson, who had been a Berkeley activist, wrote *MacBird*, a Shakespearean satire on the Kennedy assassination. At times it was difficult to know whether eliciting laughter had become more important than mobilizing anger. There is no way to prove this, but part of the success of the early New Left in attracting young people may have been the feeling that a good sense of humor made political activity not only more interesting than the lives of the organization men, but somehow less threatening than political opposition tends to be. Activists were more likely to enjoy the zest for life of colorful demonstrators than they were to worry about police violence or FBI investigation.

None of it lasted, or lasted very long. Comics themselves, for one thing, stopped adding to the fun. Bruce killed himself with drugs. Winters suffered from depression and spent two spells in a psychiatric hospital. Lehrer retired, both as a singer and as a mathematician. Gregory dropped humor for civil rights activism. Nichols and May went their separate ways. And, much later, Allen married his stepdaughter and Louis C. K. acknowledged engaging in sexual abuse. As the Vietnam War continued and little progress was evident in race relations, the left began to turn more serious. The nonviolent protests in the South gave way to racial violence in the North. People were killed during antiwar rallies on campus. Richard Nixon attacked the protestors, and Spiro Agnew scorned them. One could feel all the comic energy leaving. By 1969, it seemed to be the late Charles Manson everywhere you turned, and there was nothing humorous about him.

All of this was not simply a result of "the establishment" coming down on subversive comedy. Those attracted to the New Left turned against humor in large part because the issues with which it was concerned no longer seemed very funny; as the New Left went into a period of deep introspection about its own sexism and racism, Hoffman and Rubin became symbols of male chauvinism rather than of political protest. In matters so close to home, humor became taboo. The madcap culture of the New Left had come to resemble the self-confessional setting of Alcoholics Anonymous.

The years before and after Trump's 2016 victory did feature considerable humor in the form of television comedians who mocked politicians and took particular pleasure in mocking Donald Trump; one of them, Jimmy Kimmel, even found himself front and center in the debate over the repeal of Obamacare. As a number of studies have shown, late-night television comedians such as Jon Stewart and Stephen Colbert have had a significant impact on American politics; in particular they have appealed to younger viewers, many of whose political perspectives were shaped more by comedy than by news.[30] Their success demonstrates both that comedy is still alive in America and that it is still a force of opposition.

For all their success, however, television comedians have not been able to dull a widespread feeling that the left has lost much of its ability to laugh, Barack Obama with his brilliant comic timing and sense of irony excepted. "I'm not here to tell you some good jokes," Bernie Sanders said during a campaign stop in Iowa in 2016. "I have a bad sense of humor. It wouldn't work in any case." In this, he was correct—and also symptomatic: none of the issues Sanders brought to his campaign—class inequality, free college tuition, overturning the *Citizens United* decision of the Supreme Court—brought grins to anyone's face. Humor was as missing from a rally of Bernie Sanders as compassion was from a rally of Donald Trump. Sanders's shtick was the didactic political lecture. The same may well prove true of other potential Democratic presidential candidates in 2020.

At the heart of its problem, many critics believe, are the left's commitments to two ways of thinking that make it especially dour: identity politics and political correctness. Two liberal writers have criticized these tendencies with considerable passion, the political scientist Mark Lilla and the journalist Jonathan Chait. I am sympathetic to much of their critique; the willingness of the left to prevent conservative speakers from having their say on campus really is, as Chait puts it, a "symptom of left-wing ideological repression."[31] It is as if the left were trying to establish an exceptionally high barrier to entry, and only those willing to attack the glories of liberalism past are allowed to climb over it.

Both Chait and Lilla, however, lump together identity politics and political correctness as if they were versions of the same thing. In Lilla's words, the term "liberal" these days "is considered, with some justice, as a creed professed mainly by educated elites cut off from the rest of the country who see the issues of the day principally through the lens of identities; and whose efforts center on the care and feeding of hypersensitive movements that dissipate rather than focus the energies of what remains of the left."[32] In contrast, I would make a distinction between identity politics, which can be healthy, and political correctness, which is nearly always deadly.

Because this country has been more divided by ethnicity, race, and culture than by social class, a politics of identity strikes me as often a necessary requirement of political expression, especially for those whose group status does not, or even did not, include them in the favored majority. It is true that identity politics substitutes the interests of the group for the community as a whole, and in that way can contribute to Balkanization. But if one believes that one of America's main problems is narcissism, then group identity can at least promote a consciousness of the needs of others, even if they are similar in race, ethnicity, or gender. I view identity politics not as a form of opposition to national citizenship, as Lilla does, but as a step on the path to national citizenship. We are more likely to make citizens out of those who are already members of groups than those who go it alone.

The matter is quite different when it comes to political correctness. Donald Trump did not campaign against identity politics; in fact, he embodied it with his calls for white political identity in the face of perceived threats from minorities and immigrants. But he did run, and quite successfully, against political correctness. Much of what he said in opposition to political correctness was simply an appeal to racism, nothing more and nothing less. Nor do conservative opponents of political correctness sound very credible when they attack liberals for violating free speech without mentioning their own efforts at repressing it. As awful as political correctness is, much of the conservative criticism of it tends to be an exercise is bad faith.

The havoc wrought on American campus life by political correctness is bad enough: it presumes guilt, downplays due process of law, interferes with academic freedom, and cultivates conformity. Indeed, zealots seeking to prosecute eighteen-year-olds for saying the wrong thing about women and minorities mimic, of all people, Joe McCarthy's inquisitorial side. Worse, in the humorless world the left has helped create, practitioners of political correctness claim to know what lies in people's hearts, when it is our acts that should matter to those with whom we share a country. A sociologist who was not one of the mature liberals but shared much with them, Erving Goffman, drew attention to the backstage areas in which we practice how we will present ourselves to others. A liberal society will wall off back stages from the public gaze. Attacking people for what they think is flat-out not respectful of a liberal way of life.

On top of all this, political correctness makes for bad politics. We can apply a laugh test to determine whether we are in the presence of a demagogue: if a candidate for office never tells jokes, we are. We need a touch of humor in our leaders to help humanize them. A candidate with a dash of wit is generally one who will not take herself too seriously, who realizes that she cannot solve every problem. Gaining a little distance from the world is the best way to govern it. Puritan zealots have always been with us, and most of the time they are viewed as nosy busybodies up to no good. That instinct is a correct one. A society that has lost its taste for laughter will always be under considerable stress. No wonder so many Americans are finding politics so distressing these days. It may continue to offer excitement, even if that is debatable, but it no longer offers relief.

If William Shakespeare were alive and about to write a play dealing with the Trump years, would it be comedy or tragedy? Most likely, I would wager, neither. Donald Trump is what you get when your culture lacks both a heroic and a comic sensibility. Trump is the most literal of presidents and seeks nothing less than complete identification with what is called his base; although he speaks in front of them, he does not speak over them. He and his audience are locked together in a mutual ritual of affirming what is least noble about both: his vanity and their anger. No ambiguity, no need to have one's words interpreted, are necessary here: "Lock her up" and "Make America Great Again" do not express a complex view of the world. His rallies, as well his efforts at governing, are designed to convey a fable of oneness, in terms of his base's relationship with both him and each other. The qualities we associate with both tragic and comic great literature—self-reflection, growth, irony, ambiguity, economy of prose—have no place here. One goes to hear Trump speak not to learn but to be reaffirmed. Daniel Patrick Moynihan once spoke of defining deviance down, lowering the standard of what is considered acceptable.[33] With Trump, we are driving down not what is deviant, but what was once considered normal.

Certainly for many Americans, especially those of a more humane disposition, Trump's years in office constitute one tragedy after another. Yet Trump cannot be considered a tragic hero in the Aristotelian sense because he lacks the tragic hero's two major characteristics. First, he is not of noble birth. The opposite is in fact true: Trump's upbringing in the borough of Queens, and his resentment toward those Manhattan lifestyles that touch on royalty, furnish the defining motivations of his life. Second, Trump does not suffer from a tragic flaw. Unlike Othello's jealousy or Macbeth's abundance of ambition, he is driven by far too many flaws to focus on only one. Duplicity, hypocrisy, sexual license, grandiosity, corner cutting, refusal to apologize, moneygrubbing—any one of these would make for a great evening at the theater. Trump is more reminiscent of the Snopes family of William Faulkner's imagination than of Richard III or, as New York's Public Theater suggested, of Julius Caesar.

Trump possesses a bleak sensibility rather than a tragic one. That is why he talks often about the sorry state of the world, less so about the sorry state of America, and not at all about the sorry state of his followers. The stories of decay he relates are gruesome: vicious enemies abroad, lawless immigrants within, oppressed white people everywhere. Yet the solution—"I alone can fix it"—is upbeat. Those in Trump's base have had their share of tragedies—in fact, their worlds seem to be falling apart—but attending a Trump rally is not one of them. Not even the three major hurricanes that took place in his first year in office revealed any tragic sentiment in the president's mind. Trump overemphasized the damage caused by the first two storms, not to mobilize help for the victims, whose plight he only dimly recognized, but to express his belief that any hurricanes daring to take place on his watch could not help becoming among the greatest hurricanes of all time. He also reviewed his own efforts at hurricane relief in Puerto Rico and pronounced himself satisfied, even though Puerto Ricans were still facing disaster. Not for Trump any tragic choice between what the world needs and what he wants.

Trump's lack of a comic touch mirrors his lack of a tragic one. It is widely considered plausible that Trump decided to make a serious run for president after he was offended by the cutting humor of Barack Obama at the 2011 White House Correspondents' Dinner. Trump's rallies, both before and after his 2016 victory, have been too angry to allow for much comedy. His speaking style in its scripted moments is too stiff, and in his unscripted moments too unhinged, to allow for jokes. Trump is sarcastic, and sarcastic people are very rarely a barrel of laughs. (It is noteworthy in this regard that when Trump issues an astonishingly offensive tweet, such as the one claiming that Democratic members of Congress who did not stand and clap at his 2018 State of the Union speech were guilty of treason, he or his spokesperson responds by saying it was only meant sarcastically.) Ask one who knows: when the late-night television comic Seth Meyers, formerly of *Saturday Night Live*, questioned Senator Al Franken of Minnesota, also a former writer and performer on *Saturday Night Live*, about Trump's sense of humor, Franken answered, "I don't think he is funny at all."[34] (Nor was Franken when he turned out to have engaged in sexual harassment earlier in his career.)

Humor, as Niebuhr wrote, is a requirement for the second childhood that a mature person experiences: "It is not without significance that the real saints of history as distinguished from morbid, self-flagellating ascetics, have a delightful sense of humour, as had Francis of Assissi for instance. This sense of humour is based on a curious quality of disillusionment which has not resulted in either bitterness or despair. . . . This quality of mirthful serenity is unlike the innocency of childhood which knows no evil. It has looked into the abyss of evil and is no longer affrighted by it. This state might be termed a second childhood, but for the uncomplimentary connotations of that term. It is, at any rate, the spiritual state which follows the second birth of repentance and conversion."[35] Trump, a man totally without humor, is too busy enjoying his first childhood to commit to a second one.

If Trump's lack of a tragic sensibility has had ramifications for our politics, so has his lack of humor. Had Trump been Irish or Jewish or African American, he might have had at his disposal a rich tradition of ethnic humor passed down from one generation to another, but lacking much of any ethnicity other than whiteness, he is a man without humorous qualities. Humor, like the frontier in American history, is an outlet for frustration, a safety valve that allows leaders the space to lead and followers an opportunity to disagree. FDR's humor helped him resolve the tensions over immigrants in his time with just three words: "My fellow immigrants," as he addressed the Daughters of the American Revolution in 1938. Trump, like the many authoritarians around the world, has no such light touch at his disposal. Without the prospect of the kind of release that humor allows, severe cracks begin to appear in the edifice of politics, threatening to tear it down. No humor is available, save on late-night television, to offset the unbearable tension of the Trump years.

Since Lionel Trilling's *The Liberal Imagination* first appeared in 1950, far more attention has been paid to the second word in the title than to the third. Of the two concepts, our liberalism, for all the attacks against it, is in better condition than our imagination. American history, as another of the mature liberals, Arthur Schlesinger Jr., taught us, runs in cycles.[36] It may well be that in the future Americans will elect as president candidates even more extremist than Donald Trump, making him look like a moderate in retrospect. But it is more likely, I believe, that the country's flirtation with the humorless right will lead it once again to a faith in a more humorous left. It would not be the first time we went from one extreme to another.

As important as this issue is, however, it is not the major one we face. Our imagination needs a revival deeper and more sustained than either its liberalism or its conservatism. There is no better indication of America's political immaturity than our inability to deal with the full range of human emotions: the tragedy we feel we can never overcome and the comedy that makes it impossible to stop laughing. Our problem is not that our politicians are scripted. It is that they are reading from the wrong scripts.

6
IMMATURE DEMOCRACY

Donald Trump may not bear much resemblance to Hamlet, but there is something rotten in his—and our—state. This deeper problem is what we must address if we are to avoid electing Trump-like demagogues to the presidency in future years. That many will spring up in his wake seems all but indisputable, even if they are likely to be but pale copies of the original. Although Trump had few ties to the Republican Party before he won its presidential nomination in 2016, his fortunes and its have merged during his time in the White House. So long as the formula he developed of preaching populism to the electorate while pursuing policies beneficial to the rich continues to work, his party is likely to follow his path. Even more seriously for the future of American democracy, it has already become clear that one cannot count very much on elected Republican politicians with conscience, or what John F. Kennedy called profiles in courage, to challenge his methods. Most of the party is too preoccupied with passing its agenda to care very much about the disgrace their president brings to America. Trumpism, in one form or another, is likely to be alive long past the time when he is.

If the Democratic Party were vibrant and blessed with new ideas and leaders, Trump's capture of the Republican Party would be at least partially offset and might even turn into an advantage. But the Democrats do very little to inspire any hope. The most visible Democratic leaders are, like me, well past retirement age. The party is as torn by conflicts as ever, divided between pragmatists who believe that the best path is to appeal to independents and disaffected Republicans and those who wish to see a sharp move to the left to capture and reflect public anger. Disputes over the proper role and leadership of the Democratic National Committee have left serious scars. No one seems to have a good grasp on where the party should go, let alone how it should get there. We do know that in response to Trump's failure to denounce sexual predators surrounding him, a substantial portion of the opposition to him consists of women newly energized by the Me Too movement (#MeToo) who are likely to play a major role in the Democratic Party, including as possible presidential candidates. Nonetheless, a unified, coherent, and powerful alternative to Donald Trump has not yet emerged on the scene. Trump's unpopularity in the polls has reached historic lows, but it has not yet been transformed into positive feelings for his political opponents.

Whatever the future may bring, the question of why Americans chose Trump as their president in the first place still bears answering. Three broad strands of explanation have already emerged. One sees the main cause of Trumpism in the fact that he, his party, and his party's voters are too firmly in the clutches of racism to make liberal or humane decisions; his is a revolt of the aggrieved. The second is that he and so many of his supporters lack the knowledge that informed citizens ought to possess; his is a revolt of the ignorant. The final is that Trump is the American version of a European reaction against liberal democracy, fueled by the anger of so many of the less well-off as they find themselves redundant in a new economy, wondering what has happened to their once so promising lives, and living in fear of the foreign-born so suddenly visible all over their neighborhoods; his is a revolt of the displaced. All three explanations contain a great deal of insight. But all of them are also incomplete. To gain a fuller understanding of what Donald Trump represents, we need to return to the way the midcentury liberals reacted to the McCarthyite and radical right demagoguery of the 1950s and in particular to their emphasis on the importance of maturity.

The specter of racism has always loomed over American political behavior. It is not surprising, then, that one explanation for Trump's victory focuses on the racial resentment expressed by so many of his followers. There are two contradictory ways of talking about Trump at the present moment, and although they are seemingly contradictory, they oddly seem to work together. One is that the American electorate overcame centuries of racism when it elected Obama in 2008. The other is that racism was above all else the primary cause of Trump's victory over Obama's successor eight years later.

To gain a sense of the meaning of Trump's elevation to the presidency, a thought experiment is in order: what would America have been like if Hillary Clinton had defeated him? If she had won, I believe, our political environment would likely be far more toxic than it is under Trump, especially if the Republicans had retained one or both houses of Congress. I shudder to think what they would have done with their subpoena powers. But imagine the celebrations that a Clinton win would have produced among more liberal Americans. Not only had Americans looked past race when they elected Obama, we would have been told, but they broke the gender barrier as well by electing Clinton. The message would have been unambiguous: this is no longer a world in which only white men, most of them elderly and wearing red ties, run the country. I believe it would have been fair under such a scenario to conclude that American politics had taken a major step in the direction of maturity. This is not to praise either Obama or Clinton, though I admire both. But the election of Clinton would have indicated that at long last our country had shown itself capable of looking past race and gender to choose the best possible candidate.

Clinton, of course, did lose, and so did any idea that our country had moved past the racial and gender discrimination that has long marked our politics. If anything, Trump's victory in 2016 instead revealed how much racial resentment had been building up in the United States during the Obama years. Were we post-racial or most-racial?[1] The answer is already coming in: we are anything but post-racial. The *Washington Post* contains a space called "Monkey Cage" in which political scientists report on their current research. A considerable number of the entries posted there show how important race was in the election. Tesler himself observed the close connection that had developed in America between partisanship and race: voters who blamed the problems facing blacks on aspects of black culture vote for one party, and those who do not, vote for the other.[2] Others concluded, along similar lines, that race played a greater role in Trump's victory than authoritarianism,[3] or that whites turned out in greater numbers than blacks.[4] The results in 2016 not only shocked most of the public and the press, but sent a bevy of political scientists to work, and what they found, in studies far too numerous to be cited here, was that race played an overwhelming role in explaining Trump's win.

Why not, then, just conclude the discussion here and say that Trump was elected because the United States contains so many racists? One reason it makes little sense to do so is the paradox of Obama: how could the same American people who looked past race only eight years earlier to elect Obama choose someone who did not view him as a legitimate American? Moreover, the fact that Trump won in the Electoral College but lost the popular vote, a fact that should not question his legitimacy as president, still leaves us with the conclusion that more people rejected his racism than accepted it. Matters involving race are rarely simple, and it gains us little, although it no doubt pleases some on the left, just to conclude that Trump won because of his deeply ingrained prejudices.

There is therefore another, and perhaps more important, reason to keep the discussion going: racial attitudes may themselves be part of a larger picture that more thoroughly explains such an event as Trump's election to the presidency. Some hints of this conclusion lie in the more ethnographically based work I cited in chapter 3, on mass society. In her study of rural Wisconsinites, for example, Katherine Cramer concluded that the urban-rural divide she found in that state of course had racial components, but that such views could not help explain, to cite just one example, the deep hostility rural voters expressed toward faculty at the University of Wisconsin, most of whom are white. Race, she felt, did not play as significant a role in accounting for people's views as one might expect.[5] Arlie Hochschild's respondents in Louisiana, such as the one named Jack Hardy, were more likely to use explicitly racial language, but there too attitudes toward race were tied up with complaints about the entire direction that American society was taking. Talking to a respondent she calls Mike, Hochschild comments: "But something else animated Mike's dislike for the government, something I was to discover wherever I went. Sometimes talk of it was angry, front and central; sometimes it was quietly alluded to. But over their heads, the federal government was taking money from the workers and giving it to the idle."[6] Racism is definitely playing a role here, but it is indirect. It is not that "racism equals votes for the right." It is more that "racism equals dislike of government equals the (quite false) belief that government spends hugely on blacks equals votes for the right." Race, in this sense, stands for a general unhappiness about many other things, such as resentment toward immigrants or anger about how difficult it is to be accepted at an elite university or complaints about the way America's rural way of life is disappearing.

Other evidence complicates reliance on race as the sole reason for Trump's victory. For instance, a small but significant number of voters, somewhere between 6 and 12 percent, voted for Bernie Sanders in the primaries but Donald Trump in the general election. Sanders, however, never sought the support of white racist voters, and since Sanders did not appeal to racial themes, some other explanation must be at work here.[7] It is also the case that while racism may be a strong factor in explaining Trump, the number of hard-core racists in the country may not be all that large. Opposition to the explicit racism on display at an Alt Right rally in Charlottesville, Virginia, in August 2017 was significant, for example, and Trump did not win himself much support for coming down on the side of the racists. Economic anxiety, finally, was stirred together with racial anxiety for many people, making it close to impossible to separate out the effects of each. None of this is to deny the importance of racism in electing Trump. It is instead designed to supplement it.

If anger in general lies behind so much of the resentment we see in contemporary American politics, we find ourselves back at the beginning in our efforts to understand Donald Trump's political support: what is it that explains why so many Americans, living with relatively low unemployment, a consumer economy that puts wonders at their fingertips, and with relative peace at hand, are so angry? This is not a question that can be answered by consulting election studies or even intense ethnographic observation. Surely it has something to do what people themselves say about their views of the world: increased immigration, economic uncertainty, hatred of political correctness, or just fear of the new. But there does appear to be something going on in the background suggesting that racism, to be sure always present in American political life, is an indicator of something even deeper. If there is indeed a "deep story," it may tell no more than the tale of white Americans losing any empathy toward people different from themselves.

Perhaps the reason why Donald Trump is so ignorant of the world is that his supporters are. This supposition lies at the heart of the second explanation of the Trump victory. The American voter, it has been demonstrated many times over, suffers from a very high level of political illiteracy, or what political scientists more politely call "low-information voting."[8]

The Pew Research Center furnishes the gold standard when it comes to ascertaining how much Americans know about their political system. In a typical recent report, Pew found that only 34 percent of all Americans could pick out of five options the correct name of the chief justice of the Supreme Court, while 33 percent knew that there were three women on the court.[9] (Correct identification of the swing voter on the court, who has a disproportional influence on decisions, was made by 28 percent.) In foreign affairs, the situation was hardly better:

a minority of Americans could identify the French prime minister, or, for that matter, the United States secretary of state. And this was only the tip of the iceberg. A recent book by law professor Ilya Somin notes that in the run-up to the congressional elections of 2014, only 38 percent of Americans knew that Democrats controlled the Senate and that Republicans controlled the House, and this when sheer guessing might have yielded something closer to 50/50.[10] The political knowledge level of the average American is so abysmally low that it has become something of a game played by insiders to come up with the single most striking example—that 10 percent of us believe that Judge Judy serves on the Supreme Court, for example, or that more Americans know who Michael Jackson was than know what the Bill of Rights is—of how little about politics the American people know. Political ignorance should not be a joking matter. In America it is.

The political scientists Richard Fording and Sanford Schram have singled out low-information voting as a primary cause of the election of Donald Trump.[11] They developed a simple scale of political knowledge based on identifying the length of a US Senate term and the four items on which the government spends the least. To this they added a concept called the need for cognition (NFC): those with high NFC want to understand complex problems and spend the time necessary to do so, while those with low NFC are not very curious about the world and tend to rely on what they see on television or hear in ads. The Fording-Schram analysis of the American National Elections Studies 2016 Pilot Study showed that those who combined low information with a low need for cognition voted disproportionately for Trump. This is not a partisan finding. In 2012, Republican nominee Mitt Romney attracted far more support from knowledgeable and active Republicans than Trump did in 2016. Fording and Schram view the strong relationship between lack of knowledge and support for Trump as related to another finding: Trump voters tended to be worried about immigrants, racial minorities, and refugees. Compared to those who supported Hillary Clinton, in short, Trump supporters vote far more on the basis of their emotions, particularly the emotion of fear, than on factual knowledge.

It is not just political scientists who believe that low-information voters preferred Trump in 2016. "Donald does well with voters who have relatively low information, who are not that engaged and who are angry, and they see him as an angry voice," concluded Senator Ted Cruz of Texas, Trump's major rival for the nomination, who, despite his Ivy League credentials, competed furiously with Trump to win those low-information voters for himself and was clearly jealous that Trump had topped him.[12] Certainly Trump, fascinated by all things Trumpian, understood the basis of his appeal. After crushing Cruz in the Nevada primary in February 2016, he announced, "We won the evangelicals. We won with young. We won with old. We won with highly educated. We won with poorly educated. I love the poorly educated."[13] Trump's support certainly bore out the last of these claims: 57 percent of those with a high-school education or less voted for Trump in the Nevada primary compared to 20 percent for Cruz. The same pattern held true in the general election: according to the *New York Times* exit poll, Trump topped Clinton among those lacking a high-school degree 51 to 45 percent, while Clinton beat Trump among those with postgraduate study 58 to 37 percent.[14]

The 2016 election was so unique and unpredictable that numerous studies of it will surely be forthcoming. But the idea that Trump voters were far more likely to vote out of emotions rather than on facts is unlikely ever to be definitively challenged. Indeed, if this finding proves to be durable, it may be that the culture war between left and right will soon be replaced by one between the informed and the angry. This will not be a fun thing to watch: take intelligence to its end result and you get arrogance, and take anger to the same place and you get violence. Our politics would then remain at a stalemate, not about what we believe, which is usually called ideology, but about how we come to hold our beliefs, which calls into question the even more divisive issue of what kind of people we really are. There is a good chance that we will look back on our earlier culture war, the one involving such issues as abortion and gay marriage, as relatively peaceful compared to what lies ahead.

There is a wonderful democratic symmetry to the idea that an uninformed electorate ought to be represented by an uninformed president. But in spite of all the attention that has been given to the lack of political knowledge of the American people,[15] I nonetheless believe that low-information voting may *not* be the major reason why Donald Trump found himself elected president. There are at least four reasons why.

First, the American voter has always been poorly informed. Our political past is filled with examples of urban machines led by rapacious bosses, parties buying votes aplenty, scurrilous attacks on the character of candidates, bloc voting by ethnic groups, racial terrorism to prevent African Americans from exercising the franchise, manipulative advertising, and, lest we forget, a number of demagogues who came on the scene long before Donald Trump. James Madison pointed out that no government would be necessary for angels because he knew we weren't. Trump's ability to capture the support of the uninformed is in this sense just politics as usual. The consequences of a Trump victory may be dramatic, but the cause of it is not.

Second, Trump did appeal to feelings rather than facts, and while facts in a democracy ought to trump feelings, it is also true that feelings, however dangerous, nonetheless play a role in how people vote. For the most avid Trump supporters, it seems clear that nothing Trump does as president is likely to lower their opinion of him. Given a choice between a leader who promises that he will listen to their cries of help even while pursuing policies that will devastate them economically, they will accept the latter to obtain the former. The fact that no scandal or demonstration of political ignorance on his part, of which there is a constant flow, could change the minds of his strongest supporters is impressive, if in a perverted sort of way; theirs is a dug-in loyalty that cares not a whit for the usual ups and downs of American election campaigns. Their factual knowledge may be thin, but their emotional commitment to their candidate could not be stronger.

Democracy, furthermore, is not a quiz show: Trump's supporters believe that they have become the neglected Americans while their government gives too much support to those beneath them, and if liberals criticize them for not knowing the name of their congressman, then liberals are irrelevant to them. In 1994, the Canadian philosopher Charles Taylor argued for "a politics of recognition" among those who are slighted by the majority.[16] The Trump campaign, with its appeal to white working-class high-school graduates, is one of the most successful examples of the politics of recognition we have seen. Trump's victory has called attention to the plight of non-college-educated whites, burdened by low wages and factory closings, watching as their children become addicted to painkillers, and resentful of liberals who in their view are just snobs. Perhaps attention is all they want, and, having attained it, they are satisfied.

Third, there are some issues on which we are all low-information voters. Voters these days are increasingly called upon to decide ballot questions, and it is frequently the case that such questions are written poorly, difficult for even a retired professor of political science to figure out. There now exists, furthermore, especially in California, where initiatives are used to make policy, a ballot-industrial complex in which well-endowed firms and other interests hire professionals to write ballot initiatives (in ways favoring them), collect signatures to put them on the ballot, advertise in their favor, and organize people to vote for them. It would take a highly motivated voter with a lot of time on her hands to investigate what is really going on behind the scenes. For example, Amendment 1 on Florida's 2016 ballot "establishes a right under Florida's constitution for consumers to own or lease solar equipment on their property to generate electricity for their own use."[17] If you are in favor of switching to alternative sources of energy, this seems clearly written to get your vote. In fact, you already have the right in Florida to purchase and use solar equipment. The phrase "for your own use" is meant to prevent consumers from selling back their excess energy to the utility companies, and in that way, undermining the economic incentives for installing solar panels in the first place, clearly the reason why Florida's utility companies urged a yes vote. In a victory for informed voters, Amendment 1 was narrowly defeated.

As this example shows, ballot-initiative voters are not necessarily politically illiterate. It is often the case that voters will rely on surrogates, such as a candidate's political party or the views of talk-radio hosts, as shortcuts to a decision, but even where ballot questions contain no partisan signals and do not become fuel for culture warriors, voters can still rely on official summaries as well as advertisements to make a reasonably well-informed decision.[18] A twist was added in 2016. Colorado residents voted on a ballot initiative, strongly endorsed by football legend John Elway, to make it much more difficult to propose ballot initiatives. Its passage suggests the possibility that voters are getting fed up with the complexity of this kind of voting. (Truth be told, Colorado's biggest companies also wanted to limit ballot questions because they have to spend so much money to defeat them.) If there is a surprise here, it is that reliance on ballot initiatives has not resulted in total disaster. For all the money that vested interests pour into ballot initiatives to prevent reform, resorting to the ballot may be one of the only means of obtaining reforms, especially when state legislators meet infrequently, out of public sight, and in direct contact with lobbyists.

Finally, an emphasis on low-information voters leads some to the conclusion that uninformed people should not be allowed to vote at all—a cure for democracy far worse than the disease. Some academics attracted to libertarianism, for example, have pointed out how irrational it is to vote when one's individual vote counts for so little, concluding, in the more extreme case, that America would be better off with an epistocracy, or rule by the wise.[19] One can assemble anecdotes that seemingly support this case, such as the fact that candidates with deep voices attract greater support than those with higher ones.[20] But there is something off-kilter when the president of the United States challenges his former secretary of state, Rex Tillerson, to an IQ test, as if that had something, or even anything, to do with leadership. (The president's spokeswoman later said, predictably, that he was joking.) High IQs are not what we should expect of good citizens, just as they fail to capture the essential difference between Tillerson and Trump, which is that the former related to events in the actual world and the latter does not. Whatever this says about intelligence, our most highly educated president, Woodrow Wilson, was not as successful in office as the self-educated Abe Lincoln, let alone Washington, Jackson, and

Truman, all of whom never went to college. The psychologist Howard Gardner reminds us that intelligence comes in many forms and not, as IQ tests imply, simply in one.[21] Having "interpersonal intelligence," or being people-smart, may be far more valuable in a president than knowledge of the various electoral laws in the fifty states. The same might apply to voters. The true tragedy of 2016 may well be not that people were ignorant of what Trump would do once president but that they lacked sufficient people skills to realize what kind of a man he really was.

If this is true, all the information in the world will not help us when we are called upon to judge which of two candidates for high office is more honest, wise, tolerant, or judicious. In his 1888 masterpiece, *The American Commonwealth*, Lord James Bryce, clearly inspired by Tocqueville, commented: "The ordinary American voter does not object to mediocrity. He has a lower conception of the qualities requisite to make a statesman than those who direct public opinion in Europe have. He likes his candidate to be sensible, vigorous, and, above all, what he calls 'magnetic,' and does not value, because he has no need for, originality or profundity, a fine culture, or a wise knowledge."[22] Not much has changed in over a century. Consider that bad news if you would like to see well-informed voters, but good news if you value stability and consistency.

A third explanation for the rise of Trumpism can be found in the success of right-wing parties around the globe, especially in Western Europe. Populism, authoritarianism, nationalism—they have all been stirred together in a nasty brew in one European country after another. In part this is a by-product of the fact that the collapse of communism, both in Russia and in the former satellite countries of Europe, after a brief flirtation with democracy, led many countries to turn right, often hard right. In addition, countries on the periphery of Europe, such as Turkey, saw rapid economic growth, but that did not prevent them from turning right as well. Even long-established democracies have witnessed a startling increase in public support for right-wing parties. Some sense of the scope of this reaction can be

TABLE 1. Vote for right-wing parties in Europe in most recent elections

Country	Election	Right-Wing Party	% of vote
Austria	October 2017	People's Party	31.5
Denmark	June 2015	Danish People's Party	21.1
France	April/May 2017	National Front	33.9
Germany	September 2017	Alternative for Germany	13.0
Hungary	April 2014	Jobbik (Movement for a Better Hungary)	24.5
Netherlands	March 2017	Party for Freedom	13.1
Poland	October 2015	Law and Justice	27.6
Italy	March 2018	The League	17.3
		Five Star Movement	32.6

Sources: Based on data from Gregor Aisch, Adam Pearce, and Bryant Rousseau, "How Far Is Europe Swinging to the Right?," *New York Times*, October 16, 2017, https://www.nytimes.com/interactive/2016/05/22/world/europe/europe-right-wing-austria-hungary.html?_r=0; and Wikipedia entries for additional countries.

gleaned from table 1, which shows how well right-wing parties are doing in recent elections.

A phenomenon as broad as this one must have common causes; we are not dealing here with the particularities of one country or another. Three interrelated developments are generally put forward as responsible. The first is the breakdown of what in the years after World War II was viewed as a popular social contract that shaped the domestic politics of nearly all European countries. Rapid economic growth combined with relatively low budgets for defense enabled these countries to offer generous public benefits, such as retirement plans, subsidized childcare, and health insurance. In more recent times, significant economic growth has become harder to achieve, shrinking the funds available for all such programs. This is taking place, moreover, when rates of employment are high and those who have not been able to adapt to a new economy based on technology rather than manufacturing feel increasingly isolated. If there are few opportunities for leftist parties to provide public benefits, many voters reason, then why vote for the left?

Globalization has had a huge effect on European politics as well. The plentitude of regulations that is a by-product of the welfare state is, to some, intrusive enough, but when combined with an additional batch of regulations emanating from Brussels, where the European Parliament is located, they become unbearable. The British vote for

Brexit, often taken as evidence of Europe's lurch to the right, was fueled by charges that the disposal of tea bags, the burning of light bulbs, and the use of toasters would all have to be changed to meet European requirements. Elites, in general, view such nuisances as a small price to pay for freer movements of labor and capital. Ordinary people do not. They look not only at annoying regulations but also at boarded-up factories and declining cities and see nothing but harm. Whatever economists tell us about the benefits of free trade, it has always been a hard sell in democratic political systems and harder than ever when times are tough. With free trade's benefits becoming more difficult to appreciate, right-wing reaction seems all but inevitable.

Globalization, in turn, was accompanied by increased immigration, and the fear of the cultural changes brought about by people from other countries is the third, and surely the most important, factor contributing to the rise of the right. Strange customs, languages, religions, and attitudes toward women are not very easy for large numbers of people in the host country to accept. If the mature liberals, who at times compared the American experience to that of Europe, were suddenly reborn and traveled to the Continent, they would no longer recognize it. The diversity that immigration has supplied to Europe will go down in history as a crucial turning point equivalent to the Treaty of Westphalia or the Protestant Reformation. Something so momentous is bound to have consequences, and immigration certainly did.

Racial and religious diversity has long been a fact of life in America. In Europe, it came as a complete shock. Scandinavia, for example, like the rest of Europe, turned right, but this was not because of a crisis in the welfare state, since the New Right parties did not challenge that. Here, immigration, and only immigration, fueled the change. It surely marks a turning point when citizens of Holland and Denmark, both known for their cultural liberalism, give extensive support to right-wing anti-Islamic parties, at least in part because women, gays, and other beneficiaries of the cultural revolution of our time were frightened that deeply religious immigrants from Muslim countries would challenge rights that had been so hard to win in the first place. So deep are the problems posed by increasing immigration, let alone the nationalistic response to it, that writers from both Europe and North America are beginning to talk about "the end of Europe" or what will happen in the wake of its demise.[23]

This sharp turn to the right in both Western Europe and North America has fueled extensive research by political scientists on the nature and future of democracy. Roberto Stefan Foa and Yascha Mounk are among the leaders of this revival. In a widely cited article, they ask whether we are going through a period of "democratic deconsolidation" in which people are losing faith in democratic institutions and looking instead to irresponsible, and undemocratic, strongmen. Liberal democratic citizens, they write, have become "more cynical about the value of democracy as a political system, less hopeful that anything they do might influence public policy, and more willing to express support for authoritarian alternatives. The crisis of democratic legitimacy extends across a much wider set of indicators than previously appreciated."[24] The authors present extensive data showing that public support for democratic institutions and values is collapsing and that, most crucial in their view, younger people are increasingly politically passive and uniformed. It was once a truism of political science that democracy, once established, becomes difficult to dislodge. Considerable evidence suggests to them that this may no longer be the case. The future of democracy is anything but rosy.

Not everyone agrees with this prognosis. Critics of Foa and Mounk note that younger citizens are not nearly as turned off from democracy as the authors claim, and that on some basic requirements for democracy, such as tolerance, they are more liberal than their parents and grandparents. These critics rightly suggest that we not overreact when contemplating the future of democracy.[25] But there is also no doubt that a major shift has taken place. In Western Europe, it was long the case that left-wing and center-left parties were in power and center-right and right-wing parties in opposition. Now it is the other way around.

It is a short step from findings such as these to conclude that Donald Trump is an American version of Marine Le Pen, Geert Wilders, and the other European nationalists. The United States is certainly not immune to the factors that are generating right-wing backlash in Europe. Indeed, Canadian political scientist Paul Howe, using survey data, has suggested that Foa and Mounk's already pessimistic conclusions about the future of democracy may be too optimistic, at least for the United States. According to Howe, we are dealing not just with a crisis in political institutions, which might be reparable, but with an entire change in the political culture of democracies that would be far more difficult to set straight. Howe looked at the responses to four questions: is it permissible (1) to accept a bribe, (2) cheat on taxes, (3) wrongfully claim a benefit, and (4) avoid a transit fare? Those who believed that all four of these behavioral norms could be violated were far less likely to support democratic norms than those who did not. These findings, in Howe's words, "imply that indifferent feelings toward democracy are interlaced with a broader set of self-interested and antisocial attitudes that are present among a substantial minority of the U.S. population."[26] This in turn suggests that right-wing voters do not necessarily have authoritarian personalities. As I suggested in chapter 3, adherents to the right manage to combine their authoritarian inclinations with a wild-eyed libertarianism suspicious of anyone who presumes to tell them what they can do. It is not so much democracy that is in trouble, from such a perspective, as society itself.

At first glance, Donald Trump does seem to resemble his European counterparts. Like them, he appealed to those suffering from high rates of unemployment and social disintegration presumably caused by globalization. Trump mastered the art of us-against-them rhetoric that won right-wing European populists their high levels of support. His silence in the face of violent and extremist supporters inevitably brings up references to Europe's ugly twentieth-century history. Trump is indeed unusual, writes Fareed Zakaria in a fairly typical commentary, "but in an important sense he is not: Trump is part of a broad populist upsurge running through the Western World. It can be seen in countries of widely varying circumstances, from prosperous Sweden to debt-ridden Greece."[27]

As with the supposition that Trump won because of so many low-information voters, there is much truth to the idea that right-wing populism abroad has proceeded in lockstep with right-wing nationalism at home. At the same time, however, Donald Trump is too uniquely an American political figure to resemble too closely European demagogues. Unlike Marine Le Pen, who is following in the footsteps of her father, Jean-Marie Le Pen, the former leader of the French National Front, Trump, with the exception of his dislike of minorities domestic and foreign, seems to have come to his right-wing views opportunistically. Not only does he appear to lack any fixed ideas, but he was capable of shifting from a Manhattan liberal to a right-wing zealot because he is so good at reacting to the cheers and applause of any audience he is addressing. His opposition to Islam is not grounded in a deeply felt Christianity, as is true of some of the right-wing Catholic hostility toward Muslims, since he appears to lack any kind of religious sensibility. Trump, whose daughter and son-in-law are Jewish, lacks the furious anti-Semitism attractive to the European right. Above all else, what is most striking about Trump is not the policy positions he takes, many of which do resemble those of European right-wing politicians, but his character and personality. Trump betrays a narcissistic insecurity so extreme that it would be nearly impossible for any foreign leader, or even anyone else on the planet, to match. In short, the best way to understand Trump is to look at American demagogues in the past, not European ones in the present.

Fortunately we have at least one past demagogue who fits the bill, the one against whom the midcentury liberals fashioned their ideas, Joe McCarthy. I believe that the writers and thinkers of the 1950s and 1960s paid particular attention to precisely what we require at the present time to make sense of Donald Trump: maturity. If America's choice of Donald Trump proves anything, it is that Americans are now paying the price for our failure to treat politics as an activity for grown-ups. It follows that our only hope for a more healthy democracy, now that Trump has provided such a vivid display of a sick one, is not just to vote for one political party or another, although one of them, the Republican Party, has contributed disproportionately to our malaise. We need instead to understand why Americans can be so innovative in industry, so productive in cultural achievements, so much the dream of oppressed people everywhere looking for a fresh start, so Nobel Prize–winning in scientific achievements, so advanced in medical technologies, so talented in basketball, yet at the same time capable of electing such an ignorant and mentally unbalanced person as Donald Trump. Our most fundamental question is this: why does there exist such a huge gap between the accomplishments of the American people and the dreadful choices they make for their leaders? I look to the thinkers of a generation ago to provide some answers.

What, then, is political maturity? As with emotional or psychological maturity, political maturity implies the capacity to set one's own goals and develop appropriate and realistic means to achieve them. A politically mature person votes after a careful consideration of what is at stake both for herself and for her country. It is perfectly permissible for a politically mature person to act out of anger, but she ought to be able to communicate both to her conscience and to other people what she is angry about. A politically mature person understands that violence may be necessary but always as a last resort. She will know when an issue has been sufficiently debated. Such a person will always understand that politicians want her vote and will therefore be alert to easy promises as well as dirty tricks. A person does not have to register as an independent to be politically mature but does have to acknowledge that what passes for wisdom as a young person need not determine one's stance when older. Republicans can be as politically mature as Democrats. The same holds true among liberals and conservatives: a conservative voting for Trump is as politically immature as those liberals who not long ago voted for Ralph Nader. Politically mature people seek to be lifted up by leadership rather than to be let down by demagoguery. Voting out of conformism is not mature. Voting out of conversation is. The politically mature person feels secure about who she is and what she does; thus prepared, she does not look to politics for a sense of power and domination unavailable in other realms of life. Everyone in America knows someone who is politically mature. He is that person who loves this country and is willing to criticize it when it goes wrong, treats other people with respect, votes regularly but does not brag about it, is discerning toward politicians and parties, serves as a volunteer or contributes to charity during natural disasters, and wins respect for thoughtfulness and a sense of inclusion. You can pick out the mature person from the crowd because he is the one not screaming.

Maturity in general comes with aging. This is decidedly *not* true with respect to political maturity. Indeed the very opposite may be the case: younger voters these days are more likely to be more politically mature than older ones. (This ought not come as a complete surprise given that so many of the midcentury liberals I wrote about in the first chapter were themselves under thirty when they discovered the importance of political maturity.) It is no secret, for example, that voters who are enthusiastic supporters of Donald Trump tend to be older. Protective, frightened, not always rational, they demand smaller government while clinging to the governmental benefits that support themselves. They also tend to be far more racist than their children; indeed their children these days offer themselves as guides to their often politically confused parents. Given their age, elderly voters, not unexpectedly, focus on short-term fixes rather than long-term repairs to their political system. It is as if they have spent their entire lives pursuing their careers and raising their children, and then spend their retirement expressing their anger and frustration. The American Association of Retired People will not like what I just said. That may be one reason I have never joined the AARP.

Younger voters, on the other hand, as demonstrated by the campaigns of Bernie Sanders in the United States and Jeremy Corbyn in England, have nothing against voting for older candidates whose policies resonate with them. In accusing Barack Obama and the Democrats of being Socialists, the right-wing media have made socialism more popular among the young, no doubt a sign to many (older) critics that they have not yet grown up. Yet a favorable attitude toward socialism may be a quite responsible position when the Republicans can pass a wildly unfair tax cut with little deliberation and pander to the fears of immigration, or, in the case of England, when the elderly give strong support to Brexit. It is true that millennials, those who follow the baby boomers, are less likely to vote and possess less political literacy. But if they turned out in numbers resembling the elderly, they would constitute a voting bloc of enormous power. One of the most important questions we face, then, is not whether the young will mature politically as they age but whether the political maturity they already have will be maintained. A near-perfect example of younger Americans supplying the maturity America needs took place in the aftermath of a vicious school shooting in Parkland, Florida, in February 2018. As politicians at first responded to the shooting with tired and irrelevant excuses for no action, surviving high-school students themselves took to the streets and to the Internet to demand that serious efforts at gun control take place. As horrific as the killing was, the reaction by these young people showed a giant step in the direction of political maturity.

Maturity in politics, furthermore, cannot be forced. Either it grows because citizens become tired of acting like spoiled children or it does not. Becoming politically mature is not an obligation like jury duty. No one will punish you if you choose not to vote in a responsible manner, and some may even praise you. Australia requires every citizen to vote, but I cannot imagine a society requiring everyone to act like an adult before they exercise the franchise. A politically immature people, moreover, will not become more mature by the next election, or the one after that. After all, the mature liberals of the 1940s and 1950s, faced with the antics of Joe McCarthy, hoped that Americans of their time would be more careful in their choice of leaders. Seventy or so years later, we are still waiting.

Generally speaking, a politically mature individual will also try to be a politically informed one. Yet the one is not the same as the other. Political maturity exists not when a people can name judges on the Supreme Court, but when they treat politics and its benefits and obligations in a serious way. All it really takes for a person to become politically mature is to want to do so. Making that commitment is the difficult part. Once it has been made, the path to political maturity opens up somewhat naturally. Unlike political literacy, it does not cost money for tuition in order to again additional knowledge. It does not require you to stay up all night studying math to pass an SAT test. You need not worry if your real desire is to cut hair rather than be a librarian. Some argue, wrongly in my view, that intelligence is genetically passed on, but there is no argument whatever about the fact that political maturity is not, even if it is dependent on cultural factors that parents do pass on to their children. Political maturity develops through life as a person experiences opportunities to grow. Everyone has such experiences, rendering the capacity for political maturity universal. There is nothing amiss about a high-school dropout in Kentucky achieving a greater degree of political maturity than a tenured humanities professor in Berkeley—or vice versa. When the citizens of Arkansas elected and reelected J. William Fulbright to the Senate, they demonstrated political maturity. When Republicans of Alabama chose Roy Moore as their nominee for a Senate seat, they did not. Both were conservative, and both tolerated racial inequality, but one was a statesman and the other a guttersnipe.

As is true with respect to political knowledge, there has never been a time when the American people manifested true political maturity, although they did not do so badly when they elected Lincoln or either of the two Roosevelts, even if the first of them, Teddy, was overly boyish in his enthusiasms. It may be far too much to expect much political maturity now, although the political energy associated with younger votes is certainly encouraging. Still, pronounced immaturity will prove difficult to overcome. There is a highly demagogic faction of the Republican Party, best represented by the Freedom Caucus in the House of Representatives, that clings to the idea that compromise with the opposition means giving into Satanic temptation and that ideological purity, even if it results in gridlock, is the best way forward.

Politicians should be judged by what they do, not what they say, and, dependent on the big bucks they rake in, all too many Republicans are not about to grow into a more responsible political stance.

Nor is it clear whether the Democratic Party will avoid Trump-like rhetoric and activism in an effort to regain national power. No party has a monopoly on populistic demagoguery, and the left-wing variety is still out there waiting to be tried again and again. Still, there do exist rays of hope: Trump's total lack of maturity, by showing us every day he is in office what political maturity is not, offers lessons in what we might want in both the people and the leaders of a more grown-up society. The major question facing the Democrats is not whether they move to the left or the right, the question that nearly always monopolizes the discussion, but whether they develop responsible and achievable policies for arresting America's decline. It will profit America hardly at all if the Democrats adopt anything like the demagoguery of Trump to pass an agenda different from his. Lives in the short run might be improved, but not the prospects of a more grown-up politics.

The big, unanswered question is whether the American people will become ready to act like adults. If they do, I could easily imagine a new political alignment in this country, one that links those on the left seeking a more just society with those on the right fed up by what Trump has done to their party and their ideology. If they do not, we are likely to witness activists from two sides rallying their respective bases while huge numbers in the middle become more and more alienated from politics. Americans for too long have played a game of follow the leader. Their collective life will improve when they teach their presumed leaders a thing or two about how to get along.

One word of caution, however, should be offered before we try, like the mature liberals of the 1940s and 1950s, to help Americans grow into their political responsibilities. It took a massive depression and a devastating world war to remind the liberals of that time of the importance of politics carried out well. One has to hope that we need not experience anything like those cataclysmic events to grow out of our current petulance. To be sure, we may be threatened by catastrophic developments, such as global warming and its accompanying floods, fires, and hurricanes. There are, moreover, future dictatorships in store for us in a world in which liberal democratic values are increasingly threatened. Nuclear war, with more than one madman in control of nuclear weapons, threatens everyone. New pandemics are worrisome, as is artificial intelligence run out of control. There is, in other words, never a time when mature politics can be downplayed. My best hope is that we begin to approach our politics with greater seriousness *before* the next tragedy takes place rather than after.

7
SOME LESSONS FOR THE FUTURE

In a recent, and very short, book the historian Timothy Snyder, an expert on the horrors of the twentieth century, presented twenty lessons, such as cultivating an active private life and insisting on the truth, that he hoped people can learn from the past to avoid tyranny in the future.[1] Let me borrow from him the same manner of proposing some lessons Americans might learn from the awfulness of the Trump years to improve their chances of electing more mature politicians in the future, no matter how long it takes. In doing so, I hope the reader will give some credence to my promise that I am not trying to tilt the political scale to the right or the left. My aim is to appeal to both liberals and conservatives who understand the dangers to our society posed by our very demagogic president and his supporters. Here are the lessons I think most important.

Avoid petulance. In his *Politics*, Aristotle informed us that every virtuous form of government was capable of degenerating into an inferior alternative. Such was the case with what the ancient Greeks called polity, or a well-ordered community; its degenerate form was democracy, or rule by the mob. In our day, democracy has become established in many, but, alas, still too few, parts of the world. Now that it has become a reality, its degenerate form is easy enough to ascertain: it is petulocracy, or rule by the whiniest.

Petulance is a most unpleasant political stance. It makes demands without knowing what it really wants. Spoiled, it is content only with immediate satisfaction. Ungrateful, it is incapable of reciprocity.

Petulance responds to criticism by digging in deeper. One cannot convince the petulant that he is wrong or misguided; impervious to reason, his most characteristic response is to stomp his feet in anger and frustration. The capacity for petulance is insatiable; angry voices on radio and television always come up with one new outrage after another to inflame listeners convinced that, not matter how visible their vices, they are in reality the virtuous ones. Ready to fight, the petulant always start one. No wonder that America's politics has become so petulant. Used to being first in the world in everything, all too many Americans responded to their country's relative decline in international standing by picking up their marbles and going home; if the world does not want them, they do not want the world. They have proven themselves remarkably uninterested in facing adversity with calm determination, preferring withdrawal into what the French sociologist Émile Durkheim called anomie. One does not reason one's way out of petulance; one grows out of it. Some, alas, never do.

When in 2011 Rush Limbaugh called Barack Obama "a petulant, self-absorbed egoistic little man-child,"[2] he provided not only a remarkably accurate characterization of himself, but a drop-dead description of the president who would step into Obama's shoes. Donald Trump is the perfect president for a petulant people. His response to any quarrel is inevitably that the other guy started it. He favors tweets not because their length is limited but because he can fire them off whenever the spirit moves him. His method for dealing with ugly adversaries is to copy them as much as possible. Anything he loses must have been rigged. Those who work for him spend considerable amounts of time managing him—and not always successfully. He hurls insults in public and throws tantrums in private. It has become clear to all that waiting for Trump to grow up is like hoping that a Republican tax plan can actually benefit the middle class.

The worst Trump's opponents can do is to mimic his petulance. Time, as always, will tell. But one can at least hope that having seen petulance in Technicolor on such a big screen during the Trump years, the American people will at some point tire of it. Even the most ill-behaved child eventually grows up. There will come a time—alas, we cannot know when—when Trump's spoiled-child routine will play itself out.

Recognize the nobility of politics. It always surprises me, when I talk with my fellow Americans about politics, how readily most of them denounce politicians as corrupt and politics as unseemly. They do this in a way designed to convey the message that they are above such petty concerns, that they have thought long and hard about politics and have finally come to the conclusion, which they believe a deep one, that the only thing politicians do is to make promises they never intend to keep. They are convinced that Washington is a den of iniquity. They believe that too much money is spent on campaigns and that the campaigns themselves are too negative. It is an unexamined axiom that those serving in Congress are overpaid and in any case unworthy of what they do receive. Where, they want to know, are the great leaders of the past, the ones who rallied the American people to fight against depression at home and totalitarianism abroad?

Nothing is more immature, I believe, than such negative attitudes toward politics; those who believe that in hating politics they have achieved a higher understanding are in fact regressing. As first realized by the ancient Greeks in their conception of a polis, politics, as Hannah Arendt so often stressed, is one of the noblest of human enterprises, an efficient and beneficial way to hold a society together without one of its parts launching constant war against the others. It takes a long time, moreover, sometimes centuries, for a society to develop in such a way that politics becomes a substitute for warfare. Only people who forget how fortunate they were to have grown up in a working political system can treat politics with such disdain. They live off the capital that politics has provided without ever realizing how indebted they are to those who came before them—or how little of a healthy public life they will bequeath to their children. The United States should have a federal holiday, call it Democracy Day, to congratulate itself on making politics work—especially during those times when, in fact, it does.

Is it working now? Many believe that in recent years the quality of American politics has drastically declined, as evidenced by congressional deadlock and partisan wrangling. But that is what happens when politics is supplanted by ideology, in precisely the way Daniel Bell warned against. "Politics," Bell correctly noted, "offers little excitement."[3] As I have suggested, we certainly need a greater respect for both comedy and tragedy in our public lives. But one thing we have hopefully learned from the Trump presidency is that constant excitement—Whom will he insult next? Which of yesterday's stances will be repudiated tomorrow? Will he apologize this time? Who is the next to be fired? Can he ever be reelected?—is really a form of melodrama that makes for great television but poor democratic performance. A mature citizen understands that politics is necessary but that it cannot become everything. Like a well-running car, politics should hum in the background, enabling us to choose our leaders without needing to bring them in for checkups every two weeks or so. It would also help, as with our car, to pay what is necessary to obtain high quality. To be wise in the way of politics, be wise to those who demand too much attention. They recognize only their own needs, not yours.

Running against Washington in order to hold the most powerful job that city offers is the strangest of all the ways Americans treat politics; hating politics as they do, it is no wonder that they chose such a hateful man as Donald Trump as their leader. This detestation of the political is so odd that all the Frank Capra movies played end to end cannot help us understand it. It also gives us an indication of when American political immaturity will come to an end, which is when candidates proclaim that they want the job of president because power is a good thing that can be used to make society better. Until then, voting for president is like hiring a gardener who hates being around grass.

Trust experts. Found in the papers of the conservative British political philosopher Michael Oakeshott was a typescript essay called "Political Maturity." One of the major characteristics of political maturity, it said, was "not so much knowing what to do in an unforeseen situation, as knowing who to go to for advice. It means setting a high value on expert knowledge, on wide knowledge, and on impartiality."[4]

Oakeshott was right: knowing when *not* to assert your own opinions, but instead being able to defer to the opinions of those more knowledgeable than you, is a form of political maturity. Distrust, whether of experts, leaders, or the other guy, is deadly to democracy. The way citizens can gain trust in experts is by starting to trust them, perhaps slowly at first, but then more routinely and extensively. It is not democracy at work when the expert's views are considered equivalent, if not inferior, to those of ordinary people. It is a society misgoverned by petulance.

Contemporary Americans have been blessed with scientific and technological advances that have made it so much easier to live the kind of life one chooses. Yet all that knowledge will go to waste if the American people are too immature to realize that there are scientists who are in it not for the money or to prove their ideology, but to better the human condition; it is those who deny global warming, not those who call attention to it, who act in the pay of self-serving interests. I am not sure whether it is ignorance or immaturity to believe that Darwinian evolution is just a "theory" and therefore neither more nor less true than any other "theory," such as creationism, but it hardly matters: either does irreparable damage. Forgive the double negative, but not knowing something is not a political flaw. Insisting that you know everything is. That, in a word, is what is wrong with populism: it reduces all people to the lowest common denominator.

Impartiality, as Oakeshott also suggests, is also an important characteristic of maturity, although its meaning is often misunderstood. Impartiality does not mean being fair to all sides, as newspapers do by resorting to he-said-she-said coverage. Impartiality instead means that there is a place you can go to inform yourself and make judgments about how partial to be to one side or the other. Think of an impartial person not as one who stands above the fray of politics, but as one who believes that there is such a thing as justice and that people, through their political systems, are capable of finding it.

Do not listen to those who speak too loudly. Talk radio is a leading incubator of political immaturity in the United States. Speaking loudly, but in vulgar and juvenile language, betrays a failure to mature, among those who speak as well as those who listen. Americans will soon forget what Rush Limbaugh taught them to think about the Civil War or Pope Francis, but they will long remember his tone of hatred and bad faith. Insult and repudiation rule his day. His enemies are never misguided or mistaken; they are instead enemies, pure and simple. In treating the world as a hostile place, Limbaugh helps it become one. Those who take his word as gospel ought to learn that the kind of politics preached by Limbaugh lost its viability when the Hatfields stopped fighting the McCoys. The important thing to remember about our fellow citizens is that they are our fellows.

Limbaugh and his clones on conservative television are losing a considerable amount of their persuasiveness, not least because of their own gross sexual harassment and general nastiness. What was long evident to the liberal critics of these purveyors of political porn has now become evident to at least one former conservative talk-show host. Charles J. Sykes, who took pleasure in cataloguing the sins of the academic left, now wonders how he and so many others participated so avidly in feeding the beast that the extreme right has become. His answer lies in his feeling that there had once been a "wall that separated full-blown cranks from the mainstream conservative media." That wall, he believes, no longer exists. Paranoia, us-against-themism, and populism, he continues, have triumphed on the right, thus abandoning those, like Sykes himself, who still believe in small government and can even supply a quotation from Michael Oakeshott. The demands that all conservatives fall in line behind Trump, he writes, have become "clamorous," and the best hope for conservatives is to become contrarians, using their time in the right-wing wilderness to regain perspective and ground.[5] There was a time in the American past, quite familiar to the mature liberals of the 1950s, when people on the extreme left, such as Whittaker Chambers, shifted over to the right. Our politics will be improved when more thoughtful conservatives shift over to being even more thoughtful, wherever they end up politically.

Don't listen to those who speak too nicely. Civility is a term bandied about much these days among Trump opponents, confronted, as they are, by the toxic language Trump has made a routine part of what passes for political discourse. But as a way of thinking about politics, civility also has its dangers. Of all the mature liberals, Richard Hofstadter paid the most attention to those civic reformers called Progressives, who, for all their high-minded rhetoric, furthered a thinly veiled nativist reaction to the primarily Catholic and Jewish immigrants flooding into the cities. For the immigrants, politics was pretty much everything they had: urban political machines provided jobs, contacts, patronage, and, in the years before the New Deal, something resembling a welfare state. To take the politics out of politics, which is essentially what civility asks for, did not harm the Progressives, many of whose leaders were upper class, but it did disarm one of the primary ways immigrants could assimilate into the country's mainstream.[6] Whatever his historical accuracy—Hofstadter has attracted critics galore—he wanted to warn that seemingly apolitical movements could nonetheless possess a decidedly political agenda.

And so in our time. Much as Tocqueville observed, civic associations exist in every area of the United States and at all levels. Resolute nonpartisanship is the main characteristic of most of them; their job is to promote civic learning, better government, responsible citizenship, and moral development. Typical of them is the Institute for Civility in Government, located in Houston. "What is civility?" the institute asks on its website. The answer perfectly illustrates those who, faced with failures in their political system, seek to rise above it: "Civility is about more than just politeness, although politeness is a necessary first step," they write. "It is about disagreeing without disrespect, seeking common ground as a starting point for dialogue about differences, listening past one's preconceptions, and teaching others to do the same. Civility is the hard work of staying present even with those with whom we have deep-rooted and fierce disagreements. It is political in the sense that it is a necessary prerequisite for civic action. But it is political, too, in the sense that it is about negotiating interpersonal power such that everyone's voice is heard, and nobody's is ignored."[7] For some, such language may, in its idealism, appear moving. To me, it appears naïve. Civic reform of this type sets the standard too high, far out of the reach of ordinary people, and in that sense sets the stage for disappointment when civic reform is defeated, as it so often is. Understanding what politics can and cannot do in the real world takes a step toward greater political maturity. Preaching from the aisle does not.

There is also a case, perhaps limited but still necessary, for incivility in our politics. The fact that Donald Trump so frequently insults his opponents does not oblige his opponents to abjure insulting him. I have called Trump and his followers names—"infantile" is one I use a great deal—because that is what they are. In politics a duty to tell the truth should generally top a duty to be nice. Civility, like maturity, ought to be earned. By being civil to others, I am treating them with respect, but to be meaningful, that respect has to be earned. Those Republicans in Congress who have stood firmly behind Trump have not earned my respect, and I cannot imagine they ever will. When we reach the stage of a hard-won maturity, then we can talk honestly about civility.

Avoid any hint of conspiracy theorizing. Conspiracy theories, in Hofstadter's time, were invariably associated with the radical right. This was no doubt a correct perspective because, at the time he wrote, conspiratorial thinking appeared to be directly correlated with extremism. It was because they were so far removed from holding office that extreme right groups such as the John Birch Society accused those who were holding office, such as President Eisenhower, of being sympathetic to communism. Conspiracy thinking is the natural home for the frustrated. Out of power, they are free to construct the most powerful of fantasies.

One has to wonder in our day whether the reverse will take place. During the Trump years, the left is out of power. Will it, like yesterday's right, resort to conspiratorial thinking? I believe it already has.[8] When I began to explain to friends what this book was about, a certain hush would come over them when I talked about conspiracy theories, inevitably resulting in a question beginning with "But don't you really believe that . . ." followed by a disquisition on the Kennedy assassination, the power of big business, a repeat of the Tuskegee experiment, or the connection of vaccination to autism. There was a side of the

New Left in the 1960s and 1970s that believed that everything they were told by government was a lie, a not unreasonable position in the age of Lyndon B. Johnson, Richard Nixon, and the Vietnam War. For some, that suspicion has never gone away. It does not matter whether they dignify their suspicion with philosophical terms such as deconstruction. Their level of suspicion clogs the body politic. These days, events are bad enough. It is unnecessary to make them worse.

Do not vote for candidates who promise only good news. Politics can never give everybody everything they want. It has always been, and always will be, about the proper way to distribute limited resources. It may not make for great drama, but the beauty of politics done well is when everyone comes away with a little something more, but no one experiences a dramatic loss. To participate maturely in politics is to know that a candidate who never delivers bad news cannot be up to any good. If you think you will get the moon, you are unlikely to get anything.

No example of political immaturity was more striking than Donald Trump's relentless insistence that everything he would do, like everything he had already done, was not only for the best but was the best, although the populistic promises offered in 2016 by Bernie Sanders came close. Americans would never believe such wildly inflated claim-making if it came from a used-car salesman. But a surprising number of Americans actually believed Trump when he said that he would drain the swamp—and still believed him even when it had become manifestly clear that he cannot. Against this, a political scientist is rendered speechless. Americans may express high levels of distrust, but their naïveté is one of the most astonishing things about them. Here is where a touch of skepticism, but one that does not turn into suspicion, will help them better choose their candidates for office. There is no reason why frank talk has to disappear from all campaigning for office.

Admire and learn from political debates. It is a commonplace of contemporary politics that televised presidential debates, a routine aspect of American political campaigns since 1960, are superficial, unable to provide the clues people need to make an important decision, and a waste of precious airtime. Candidates from all points on the ideological spectrum essentially memorize their opening and closing remarks, the critics point out, and then stick as closely as possible to scripts designed to avoid any controversy. As in the conventions, everything that can be stage-managed is. The major objective of the participants is not to "win" the debate, whatever that means, but to avoid any televised gaffes. No wonder discontent is widespread. Writing in the flagship conservative magazine, *National Review*, Kevin Williamson said: "That some part of this republic's well-being should be dependent upon a ceremonial exchange of words between Hillary Rodham Clinton and Donald Trump—two of the most dishonest, vapid, and empty human-shaped things in American public life—is enough to induce despair."[9] "Let's call the whole thing off," the liberal Bill Moyers wrote with Michael Winship in a similar mood. "We mean the presidential debates—which, if the present format and moderators remain as they are, threaten an effect on democracy more like Leopold and Loeb than Lincoln and Douglas."[10]

This is the kind of high-minded and presumably civically responsible tone that aims to make voters feel guilty for their lack of substance. It is also off base. The debates that enabled Trump to beat his many rivals, and Hillary Clinton to triumph over her main one, and then in turn helped Trump defeat Clinton, were as informative as debates can be. It was not the candidates' respective command of fact that gave voters signals that might help them to choose between the candidates, but their respective maturity. No one watching the presidential campaign of 2016 could reasonably conclude that Donald Trump was as honest as Jimmy Carter, as free of corruption as Barack Obama, or as good a family man as Mitt Romney. When Trump loomed over Hillary Clinton as if he were stalking her in one of their debates, it gave viewers far more information about his attitude toward women than anything said by Ivanka Trump in support of working women. The media gave so much attention to the belittling nicknames Trump stuck on his opponents—"Lying Hillary," "Little Marco," "Pocahontas"—that one could be forgiven for not remembering that for most people, derogatory name-calling ends on the first day of high school. Those who voted for Trump despite all this were sending a loud and clear message that the maturity of a candidate mattered little to them. So long as that remains the case, it is impossible to rule out the future election of a candidate even more immature than this one. We need our political debates so that we might learn from them.

Pay as much respect to informal norms as to binding laws. As astonishing as it may sound, Donald Trump's clear violation of the Constitution's emoluments clause, let alone numerous other constitutional misdeeds, may not be the worst aspect of his presidency. Nor, depending on what special counsel Robert Mueller finds, will be his breaking of the law. Political norms are fully as important as laws or constitutional provisions and may be even more important.[11]

Donald Trump broke the norm that candidates for president release their tax returns. As president, he treated conventions regarding nepotism with disdain, refused to accept the independence of the Justice Department, blithely continued to use his office to generate further profits for his businesses, and lied so prodigiously that the term "lying" is no longer sufficient when applied to him. The list goes on and on. In fact, a catalogue of all the norms Trump has broken begins to sound like the statement of grievances against King George that appear in the Declaration of Independence. Not only is Trump a norm breaker; moreover, he seems to relish it, as if to remind his opponents just how little power they have to stop him.

To some, norms are fuzzy and easily violated and therefore ought to be transformed into more binding strictures, much as the norm that the presidency should be limited to two terms, once broken by Franklin Delano Roosevelt, then became embodied in the Constitution. But precisely became norms do not have enforcement power behind them, they testify to the strength or weakness of a political system. We know that politics works when leaders with enormous power limit their own power in deference to an unwritten norm; that is what kept the British political system working for centuries. Breaking a norm is a breach of trust, and trust is necessary for politics to function. One never really knows that a norm is working until it is breached. However unpunishable the breaking of a norm may be, the norm itself reminds us why democracies are better than dictatorships: we do not need to fear the powers our leaders will accumulate, and therefore we do not need to legislate them out of existence. Norms, in that sense, are remarkable things. Norms surround any office and make it worthy. That should never be taken lightly.

Treat threats properly. If you had asked me a decade ago whether the United States would ever relax tensions with Russia, I would have thought it unlikely because the American left is so weak. I would never have imagined that softness to Russia would take place because the American right would become so strong.

It is a frequent occurrence in politics to exaggerate threats in order to capture votes; an American presidency without threats is impossible to imagine. This historical pattern is so deep that it has clearly influenced the Trump administration, which has focused on the threat posed by the development of North Korean nuclear weapons, even while opposing a treaty that limits Iran from obtaining them. The oddity of Trump's approach lies not in its inconsistency, although it is remarkably inconsistent, but in his frequent allegations about how awful the United States has become—teeming with lawless streets and infested with illegal immigrants—combined with his refusal to criticize Russia for much of anything. It is as if Trump possesses a gene that causes him to see threats but gets backward where they originate. On this, moreover, he has carried his party with him. Republicans who once saw the Russians coming everywhere now have turned a blind eye to Russia's invasion of our elections, about as serious a threat to the integrity of our democracy as one can imagine.

Can't we for once get our threats straight? Many on the left, once sympathetic to Russia when it was Communist, continue their sympathy now that it has become semi-Fascist. The *Nation*'s Stephen F. Cohen, for example, counters arguments that Russia has annexed Ukraine or interfered with US elections by responding that we do or have done the same thing, or far worse, to them.[12] Meanwhile conservatives such as David Frum, Jennifer Rubin, Eliot Cohen, and Max Boot, courageous writers all, continue to warn against Russian intentions but have to put themselves in opposition to the Republican Party to do so. It is a truism that politics makes for strange bedfellows, but this is stranger than fiction. It is extremely dangerous for any country, including a democratic one, to feel threatened but not to know where the threat comes from. The danger, of course, is that if one responds to the false one, the true one will become worse.

Treat every vote as if the future of democracy depends upon it. Because it does. There were times, and not that long ago, when people on both the left and right dismissed America's parties as Tweedledum and Tweedledee. One party might spend a little less on New Deal programs and a little more on defense, while the other would do the opposite, but it hardly seemed to matter much. In the first election in which I took part, Kennedy seemed full of hope while Nixon did not, but with historical retrospect the differences between them may not have been as stark as I had thought. It is true that in the wake of Kennedy's death, Lyndon Johnson was able to obtain major domestic legislation, much of which has remained on the books until today, but it is also true that Nixon liked to surprise people by embracing the views of his opponents. Even when Americans chose Ronald Reagan as president, my initial reaction was that his presidency would be a catastrophe; while I still think that his was a failed presidency, catastrophic it was not. We survived and have continued to rely on periodic elections to choose our leaders without any of them, at least since the middle of the nineteenth century, threatening the end of the Republic.

My failures at predicting catastrophes in the past should lead me not to assume one now. But Donald Trump is unlike any other president we have ever had, and the Republican Party as presently constituted is unlike any other party. Even if the country survives Trump with little changed, perhaps the most optimistic scenario at this point, the lesson ought to be learned that democracy is at stake every time we go to the polls. This is especially the case now because of the success of nationalistic and populistic parties in the world's other major democracies. We seem to have reached an important turning point where political arrangements that did a fairly good job at maintaining peace and delivering prosperity for a generation are being put under enormous pressure. It will always constitute a crisis when Americans elect the wrong man, but to call this one "wrong" is to offer an undeserved compliment. He is more than wrong. He is a disaster.

In their thoughtful book trying to explain Trumpism, E. J. Dionne, Norman J. Ornstein, and Thomas E. Mann, a veritable dream team of DC observers, while understanding the threat that Trump poses to democracy, remain cautiously optimistic that reforms of our democracy might help the country regain its footing.[13] They offer a wide variety of suggestions, including making voting easier, reviving civil society, changing the Electoral College, reining in partisan gerrymandering, revising the calendar used by the House of Representatives, reforming the filibuster, and regulating campaign finance again. All these reforms would be valuable to implement. Yet these writers miss a key aspect of our contemporary dilemma: *politics alone cannot change our politics*. All the reforms in the world will have minor effects so long as Americans continue to treat politics as immaturely as they currently do.

Count me, then, as a pessimist on the issue of political reform, at least in the short term. The fact that a politician who has no historic ties to the Republican Party can bring the entire party with him into what the writer Kurt Andersen has called "Fantasyland" is shocking.[14] It is not made any better when people who resemble Fascists, and in one case actually was a Hungarian Fascist, work in the White House instead of inhabiting the nuttier corners of the land. If one's goal is to destroy America, the far reaches of the extreme right are far more dangerous than the Weathermen, the Black Panthers, and any other left-wing extremists from the 1960s all added together. Trump's so-called base, finally, may not make for a majority, and Trump's popularity has fallen to drastic lows in the polls, but even 30 percent support for this man is far too high. Changing the filibuster rules in the Senate is not going to exercise much influence over that.

I do not have and will not advocate one side or the other in the debate within the Democratic Party over its proper response to Trumpism, even if my invocation of the mature liberals of the 1940s and 1950s reveals my more centrist proclivities; I am not a political strategist and have no plans to become one. America may well be a center-right nation, and any Democrat too far to the left may be destined to lose. Or Americans may have become more radicalized by the Trump years and may want to hear more about protecting immigrants, improvements to health-care coverage, or a lesser role for America abroad. The future will determine all that. Let the future have its say. From where I sit, the most important question facing the Democratic Party is not the short-term issue of how it wins the presidency or the Congress the next time around, only again to lose one or the other the time after that. If the Trump years are a turning point, the turn will take time, and Democrats ought to be ready when it completes the cycle.

I do, however, want to comment on the tone the Democratic Party adopts in the post-Trump years. I believe it should avoid populism; that is evident from this book. Whatever Democrats advocate, they should do so thoughtfully. They should not be seduced by code words or shortcuts. They should recognize that a substantial number of Americans, perhaps a majority in the not-so-distant future, are secure enough to be told that they cannot have everything they want. Concepts such as compromise and trade-offs should not be over the head of most Americans. Years of extremism will soon, if they have not already, convince them that there is virtue in balance. If the Democrats turn to a more left-wing candidate next time, I hope that the overall political maturity of younger voters will help such a candidate to avoid simplistic bromides that they could never fulfill and concentrate on policies and programs that tap newer protest sensibilities than those associated with William Jennings Bryan. Likewise on the other side of the inner-party divide. A candidate that continues in the Obama/Clinton tradition is more likely to know well the responsibilities associated with a mature politician, yet he or she is likely to lack the fire and sense of outrage that Trump has instilled in so many of those who are offended by everything about him. Donald

Trump has already wreaked such destruction on the American way of doing politics—its unspoken norms, rules of fairness, decorum, and language and conduct—that all politicians in the post-Trump period will have to start all over again to repair the damage. However they try to do so, they must, at least in my view, begin to treat the American people as fellow adults, neither pandering to their lowest instincts as the Republicans are wont to do, nor, as the Democrats all too often do, insulting their intelligence with promises too good to be fulfilled. There are fine lines to be walked here, perhaps so fine that no one will be able to walk them. I hope I am wrong.

One of those German émigrés who ended up in Los Angeles in the years after World War II was anything but a mature liberal. The playwright and poet Berthold Brecht was a Socialist who generally expressed nothing but disdain for other intellectuals who did not agree with his radical views. Disliking pretty much everything about Southern California, Brecht returned to Germany after the war, only he chose, perhaps for reasons only he knows, to live in the East. Although he wrote no more plays before his death in 1956, in his poem "The Solution" he did respond to a statement of the East German government that it had lost confidence in the people:

> Would it not be easier
> In that case for the government
> To dissolve the people
> And elect another?

Brecht's widely quoted lines are cited often to remind people of the horrors of a government as awful as the one that existed in East Germany. For that reason, they appeal to people with a populistic sensibility, those who distrust authority and believe that, whatever mistakes the people might at times make, their will is always preferable to the sheer power of autocrats. I am not a fan of Brecht's political views, neither when he defended Stalinism nor when, as in "The

Solution," he turned against it. Nor am I equating the Trump years, bad as they have been, to those of the government of East Germany. Nonetheless, Brecht's words, as clever as they are, might be taken with a grain of salt, at least as they apply to America. When one looks at the rapport between the infantile Trump and so many of his politically immature followers, replacing the people may be out of the question, but asking the people to grow up does not seem unreasonable. There, I believe, lies the key to a politics capable of avoiding the worst of the Trump years.

NOTES

Chapter One

1 Charles Krauthammer, "Demagoguery 101," *Washington Post*, May 12, 2001, https://www.washingtonpost.com/opinions/demagoguery_101/2011/05/12/AFu6CV1G_story.html?utm_term=.ccdf495724d7; I am grateful to Megan Garber, "What We Talk about When We Talk about Demagogues," *The Atlantic*, December 10, 2015, https://www.theatlantic.com/entertainment/archive/2015/12/what-we-talk-about-when-we-talk-about-demagogues/419514/. See also Michael Signer, *Demagogue: The Fight to Save Democracy from Its Worst Enemies* (New York: Palgrave Macmillan, 2009).

2 Aristide Zolberg, "Moments of Madness," *Politics and Society* 2 (March 1972): 183–207.

3 *The Politics of Aristotle*, ed. and trans. Ernest Barker (New York: Oxford University Press, 1962), 215.

4 Alexander Hamilton, "Concluding Remarks," *Federalist Papers*, https://www.gutenberg.org/files/1404/1404-h/1404-h.htm.

5 Alexis deTocqueville, *Democracy in America*, Phillips Bradley Edition (New York: Knopf, 1966), 2:102.

6 C. Wright Mills, *The Power Elite* (New York: Oxford University Press, 1956), 25.

7 Daniel Boorstin, *The Genius of American Politics* (Chicago: University of Chicago Press, 1953).

8 Boorstin, *Genius*, 152.

9 John Higham, "The Cult of the American Consensus: Homogenizing Our History," *Commentary*, February 1959, 93–100.

10 David M. Oshinsky, *A Conspiracy So Immense: The World of Joe McCarthy* (1983; New York: Oxford University Press, 2005), 54.

11 Oshinsky, *Conspiracy*, 78, 145, 174.

12 Louis A. Coser, *Refugee Scholars in America: Their Impact and Their Experiences* (New Haven: Yale University Press, 1984), 85.

13 I found very useful Stuart Jeffries, *Grand Hotel Abyss: The Lives of the Frankfurt School* (London and New York: Verso, 2016).

14 Ira Katznelson, *Desolation and Enlightenment: Political Knowledge after Total*

War, Totalitarianism, and the Holocaust (New York: Columbia University Press, 2003), 113.

15 The economist Paul Krugman's critical comments about the Republican Party were offered more as an op-ed columnist than as an economics professor.

16 Daniel Drezner, *The Ideas Industry: How Pessimists, Partisans, and Plutocrats Are Transforming the Marketplace of Ideas* (New York: Oxford University Press, 2017).

17 Brad Amburn, "The World's Top 20 Public Intellectuals," *Foreign Policy*, October 7, 2009, http://foreignpolicy.com/2009/10/07/the-worlds-top-20-public-intellectuals. Mahmood Mamdani, who teaches at Columbia University, was listed as a Ugandan.

18 Lisa McGirr, *The New Suburban Warriors: The Origins of the New American Right* (Princeton: Princeton University Press, 2001), 148.

19 See Mary S. McAuliffe, *Crisis on the Left: Cold War Politics and American Liberals, 1947–1954* (Amherst: University of Massachusetts Press, 1978).

20 Michael Kazin, *The Populist Persuasion: An American History* (Ithaca: Cornell University Press, 1998), 192.

21 To be fair, Nathan Glazer later changed his mind. See his *We Are All Multiculturalists Now* (Cambridge, MA: Harvard University Press, 1998).

22 Noam Chomsky, "Reinhold Niebuhr," *Grand Street* 6 (Winter 1987): 212. For the comment on war criminals, see "On Responsibility, War Guilt and Intellectuals: Noam Chomsky Interviewed by Gabriel Matthew Schivone," Counterpunch, August 3, 2007, https://chomsky.info/20070803.

23 Reinhold Niebuhr, "The Myth of World Government," March 16, 1946, in Elisabeth Sifton, ed., Reinhold Niebuhr, *Major Works on Religion and Politics* (New York: Library of America, 2015), 660.

24 Richard Hofstadter, "Pseudo-Conservatism Revisited," in Daniel Bell, ed., *The Radical Right* (Garden City, NY: Anchor Books, 1964), 101.

25 Arthur Schlesinger Jr., *The Vital Center: The Politics of Freedom* (Boston: Houghton Mifflin, 1948), 222.

26 Arthur M. Schlesinger Jr., "Rating the Presidents: Washington to Clinton," *Political Science Quarterly* 11 (Summer 1997): 179–90.

27 Richard Hofstadter, *The American Political Tradition and the Men Who Made It* (1948; New York: Vintage Books, 1989), 250.

28 Richard Wright, *Black Boy: A Record of Childhood and Youth* (New York: Harper and Brothers, 1945); "Richard Wright," in Richard Crossman, ed., *The God That Failed* (1949; New York: Harper Colophon, 1963), 115–70.

29 Ta-Nehisi Coates, *Between the World and Me* (New York: Spiegel and Grau, 2015); Ta-Nehisi Coates, *We Were Eight Years in Power: An American Tragedy* (New York: OneWorld, 2017).

30 Paul Roazen, "Louis Hartz's Teaching," *Virginia Quarterly Review*, Winter 1998, http://www.vqronline.org/essay/louis-hartz%E2%80%99s-teaching.

31 Louis Hartz, *The Liberal Tradition in America: An Interpretation of American Political Thought since the Revolution* (San Diego and New York: Harcourt, Brace, 1955), 308.

32 Lionel Trilling, "On the Teaching of Modern Literature," in Lionel Trilling,

The Moral Obligation to Be Intelligent: Selected Essays (Evanston: Northwestern University Press, 2008), 390.

33 Daniel Bell and Irving Kristol, "Editorial: What Is the Public Interest?," *The Public Interest* 1 (Fall 1965): 4.

34 Stanley Fish, *The Trouble with Principle* (Cambridge, MA: Harvard University Press, 1999).

35 Daniel Bell, ed., *The New American Right* (New York: Criterion Books, 1955). My citations in this book refer to the revised edition: Daniel Bell, ed., *The Radical Right* (Garden City, NY: Anchor Books, 1964).

36 Richard Hofstadter, *The Age of Reform: From Bryan to FDR* (New York: Knopf 1955).

37 Daniel Bell, "The Dispossessed," in Bell, *Radical Right*, 1–45; and Bell, "Interpretations of American Politics," in Bell, *Radical Right*, 61.

38 Joseph R. Gusfield, *Symbolic Crusade: Status Politics and the American Temperance Movement* (Urbana: University of Illinois Press, 1963).

39 David Riesman and Nathan Glazer, "The Intellectuals and the Discontented Classes," in Bell, *Radical Right*, 108.

40 Seymour Martin Lipset, "The Sources of the 'Radical Right,'" in Bell, *Radical Right*, 369.

41 Richard Hofstadter, "The Pseudo-Conservative Revolt," in Bell, *Radical Right*, 95.

42 Hofstadter, *Age of Reform*, 14.

43 David Riesman, *Abundance for What?* (1964; New Brunswick, NJ: Transaction, 1993), 306.

44 Daniel Bell, "The Mood of Three Generations," in *The End of Ideology* (Glencoe: The Free Press, 1960), 286–99.

45 Lionel Trilling, *The Liberal Imagination: Essays on Literature and Society* (New York: Viking Press, 1950); Edward A. Shils, *The Torment of Secrecy: The Background and Consequences of American Security Policies* (Glencoe: The Free Press, 1956).

46 Bell, *End of Ideology*, 287.

47 Fritz Stern, *The Politics of Cultural Despair: A Study in the Rise of German Ideology* (Berkeley: University of California Press, 1961).

48 Hofstadter, *Age of Reform*, 15.

49 Irving Kristol, "Civil Liberties, 1952: A Study in Confusion," *Commentary*, March 1952.

50 Richard Gillam, "Richard Hofstadter, C. Wright Mill, and the 'Critical Ideal,'" *American Studies* 47 (Winter 1978): 85.

51 Edward Shils, "Imaginary Sociology," *Encounter* 14 (1960): 78. See also Shils, "Professor Mills on the Calling of Sociology: The Sociological Imagination of C. Wright Mills," *World Politics* 13 (July 1961): 600–621.

52 Mills, *Power Elite*, 310–11.

53 Daniel Bell, "The End of Ideology in the West: An Epilogue," in Bell, *Radical Right*, 372.

54 René Wellek, "The Literary Criticism of Lionel Trilling," *New England Review* 2 (Autumn, 1979): 26.

55 For an argument that Trilling was not "a close reader of texts," see Louis

Menand, "Regrets Only: Lionel Trilling and His Discontents," *New Yorker*, September 29, 2008, http://www.newyorker.com/magazine/2008/09/29/regrets-only-louis-menand. For a defense of Trilling by a prominent nonacademic intellectual, see Adam Kirsch, *Why Trilling Matters* (New Haven: Yale University Press, 2011).

56 John F. Kennedy, "Commencement Address at Yale University, June 11, 1962," The American Presidency Project, http://www.presidency.ucsb.edu/ws/?pid=29661.

57 Arthur Schlesinger Jr., *A Thousand Days: John F. Kennedy in the White House* (Boston: Houghton Mifflin, 1965), 105.

58 His best-known book was Eric F. Goldman, *Rendezvous with Destiny: A History of American Reform* (New York: Knopf, 1952).

59 McGirr, *Suburban Warriors*, 91.

60 Thomas B. Edsall, "How Fear of Falling Explains the Love of Trump," *New York Times*, July 20, 2017.

61 "President Barack Obama's Inaugural Address," https://obamawhitehouse.archives.gov/blog/2009/01/21/president-barack-obamas-inaugural-address.

Chapter Two

1 Michael Signer, *Demagogue: The Fight to Save Democracy from Its Worst Enemies* (New York: Palgrave Macmillan, 2009), 40–41.

2 I found the following books extremely helpful: Jan-Werner Müller, *What Is Populism?* (Philadelphia: University of Pennsylvania Press, 2016); Cass Muddie and Christòbal Rovira Kaltwasser, *Populism: A Very Short Introduction* (New York: Oxford University Press, 2017); and William Galston, *Anti-Pluralism: The Populist Threat to Liveral Democracy* (New Haven, CT: Yale Univeristy Press, 2018).

3 John B. Judis, *The Populist Explosion: How the Great Recession Transformed American and European Politics* (New York: Columbia Global Reports, 2016).

4 Ernesto Laclau, *On Populist Reason* (London: Verso, 2005), 206.

5 Rob Riemen, *To Fight against This Age: On Fascism and Humanism* (New York: Norton, 2018).

6 J. Eric Oliver and Wendy M. Rahn, "Rise of the Trumpenvolk: Populism in the 2016 Election," *Annals of the American Academy of Political and Social Science* 667 (2016): 189–206.

7 Glenn Greenwald, "What's Worse: Trump's Campaign Agenda or Empowering Generals and CIA Operatives to Subvert It?," The Intercept, August 5, 2017, https://theintercept.com/2017/08/05/whats-worse-trumps-campaign-agenda-or-empowering-generals-and-cia-operatives-to-subvert-it/.

8 Cory Doctorow, "Trump and Brexit Are Retaliation for Neoliberalism and Corruption," BoingBoing, November 10, 2016, http://boingboing.net/2016/11/10/trump-and-brexit-are-retaliati.html.

9 See Susi Merit and Birte Siim, "Gender, Populism, and Politics of Belonging: Discourses of Right-Wing Populist Parties in Denmark, Norway, and Austria," in Birte Siim and Monika Mokre, eds., *Negotiating Gender and Diversity in an Emergent European Public Space* (London: Palgrave Macmillan, 2013), 78–96.

10 Quoted in Robert Draper, "Trump versus Congress: Now What?," *New York Times Magazine*, March 26, 2017, https://www.nytimes.com/2017/03/26/magazine/trump-vs-congress-now-what.html?_r=0.

11 Publius Decius Mus, "The Flight 93 Election," *Claremont Review of Books*, September 5, 2016, https://www.claremont.org/crb/basicpage/the-flight-93-election/

12 Rosie Gray, "The Populist Nationalist on Trump's National Security Council," *The Atlantic*, March 24, 2017, https://www.theatlantic.com/politics/archive/2017/03/does-trumps-resident-intellectual-speak-for-his-boss/520683.

13 John Hicks, *The Populist Revolt: A History of the Farmers' Alliance and the People's Party* (Minneapolis: University of Minnesota Press, 1931).

14 Michael Kazin, *The Populist Persuasion: An American History* (Ithaca: Cornell University Press, 1998), 29.

15 Kazin, *Populist Persuasion*, 38.

16 "Bryan's 'Cross of Gold' Speech: Mesmerizing the Masses," History Matters, http://historymatters.gmu.edu/d/5354/.

17 Michael Kazin, *A Godly Hero: The Life of William Jennings Bryan* (New York: Knopf, 2006), 302.

18 "Text of the Closing Statement of William Jennings Bryan at the Trial of John Scopes, Dayton, Tennessee, 1925," http://www.csudh.edu/oliver/smt310-handouts/wjb-last/wjb-last.htm.

19 Quoted in Kazin, *Godly Hero*, 302.

20 Richard Hofstadter, *The American Political Tradition and the Men Who Made It* (1948; New York: Vintage Books, 1973), 246.

21 Hofstadter, *American Political Tradition*, 261.

22 See, for example, Norman Pollock, "Hofstadter on Populism: A Critique of 'The Age of Reform,'" *Journal of Southern History* 16 (November 1960): 478–500; and Lawrence Goodwyn, *Democratic Promise: The Populist Moment in America* (New York: Oxford University Press, 1976).

23 Daniel Bell, "The Dispossessed," in Daniel Bell, ed., *The Radical Right* (Garden City, NY: Anchor Books, 1964), 3.

24 Seymour Martin Lipset, *Political Man: The Social Bases of Politics* (Garden City, NY: Anchor Books, 1960), 13, 170–72.

25 David Riesman and Nathan Glazer, "The Intellectuals and the Discontented Classes," in Bell, *Radical Right*, 112.

26 Victor Ferkiss, "Populistic Influences on American Fascism, *Western Political Quarterly* 10 (June 1957): 350–73.

27 Lipset, *Political Man*, 77, 170.

28 Laclau, *On Populist Reason*, 206.

29 This, at least, is the conclusion I draw from Google Trends. See https://trends.google.com/trends/explore?q=extremism.

30 "Republican Party Platform of 1964, July 13, 1964," The American Presidency Project, http://www.presidency.ucsb.edu/ws/?pid=25840.

31 Kevin Connolly, "Grandfather of Populism Poujade Who Shook France and Changed the World," BBC News, December 2, 2016, http://www.bbc.com/news/world-europe-38370962.

32 Bell, "The Dispossessed," 2.

33 Daniel Bell, *The End of Ideology* (Glencoe: The Free Press, 1960), 294–95.

34 Müller, *What Is Populism?* 11.
35 Hofstadter, *American Political Tradition*, 244–45.
36 Richard Hofstadter, *Anti-Intellectualism in American Life* (New York: Knopf, 1963), 270.
37 Bell, *End of Ideology*, 106–7.
38 Bell, "Interpretations of American Politics," in Bell, *Radical Right*, 42.
39 Riesman and Glazer, "The Intellectuals and the Discontented Classes," 137.
40 Riesman and Glazer, "The Intellectuals and the Discontented Classes," 132.
41 See Edwin R. Bayley, *Joe McCarthy and the Press* (Madison: University of Wisconsin Press, 1981), 39–65.
42 Bryan Hardin Thrift, *Conservative Bias: How Jesse Helms Pioneered the Rise of Right-Wing Media and Realigned the Republican Party* (Gainesville: University of Florida Press, 2014).
43 Julian Sanchez, "Epistemic Closure, Technology, and the End of Distance," Blog, *Julian Sanchez*, April 7, 2010, http://www.juliansanchez.com/2010/04/07/epistemic-closure-technology-and-the-end-of-distance.
44 Hannah Arendt, *Between Past and Future: Exercises in Political Thought* (New York: Viking Compass, 1968), 227–64.
45 Hannah Arendt, *Men in Dark Times* (New York: Harcourt, Brace and World, 1968).
46 James Burnham, *The Machiavellians: Defenders of Freedom* (New York, John Day, 1943).
47 Max Weber, "Politics as a Vocation," in Hans Gerth and C. Wright Mills, eds., *From Max Weber: Essays in Sociology* (New York: Oxford University Press, 1946), 116, 121.
48 Weber, "Politics as a Vocation," 115–16, 124–25, 128.
49 Bell, *End of Ideology*, 288–89.
50 I am grateful to David Greenberg, "Richard Hofstadter's Tradition," *The Atlantic*, November 1998, https://www.theatlantic.com/magazine/archive/1998/11/richard-hofstadters-tradition/377296/.
51 Reinhold Niebuhr, "The Christian Church in a Secular Age," in *The Essential Reinhold Niebuhr: Selected Essays and Addresses* (New Haven: Yale University Press, 1986), 82.
52 Reinhold Niebuhr, *Moral Man and Immoral Society*, in Elisabeth Sifton, ed., Reinhold Niebuhr, *Major Works on Religion and Politics* (New York: Library of America, 2015), 248.
53 Dietrich Bonhoeffer, *The Cost of Discipleship* (1937; New York: Touchstone, 1995), 43.
54 Reinhold Niebuhr, *Leaves from the Notebook of a Tamed Cynic*, in *Major Works*, 125.
55 C. Vann Woodward, *Tom Watson, Agrarian Rebel* (New York: Macmillan, 1938).
56 Richard Hofstadter, *The Age of Reform: From Bryan to FDR* (New York: Vintage, 1955), 66–67.
57 Christopher Lasch, *The Culture of Narcissism: American Life in an Age of Diminishing Expectations* (New York: Norton, 1979).
58 "Populist Party Platform of 1892, July 4, 1892," The American Presidency Project, http://www.presidency.ucsb.edu/ws/index.php?pid=29616.

59 Laura Grattan, *Radical Grassroots Democracy in America* (New York: Oxford University Press, 2016), 11.

60 Michael Wolff, *Fire and Fury: Inside the Trump White House* (New York: Henry Holt, 2018), 9–18.

61 Vachel Lindsay, "Bryan, Bryan, Bryan, Bryan," https://www.poemhunter.com/best-poems/vachel-lindsay/bryan-bryan-bryan-bryan/.

Chapter Three

1 Frances Milton Trollope, *The Domestic Manners of the Americans* (1832; Peterborough, ON: Broadview Press, 2015); Bernard-Henri Lévy, *American Vertigo: Traveling America in the Footsteps of Tocqueville* (New York: Random House, 2006).

2 Edward Shils, *The Virtue of Civility: Selected Essays on Liberalism, Tradition, and Civil Society* (Indianapolis: Liberty Fund, 1997), 57.

3 Dwight Macdonald, *Against the American Grain: Essays on the Prospects of Mass Culture* (1962; New York: Da Capo, 1983), 62–63.

4 Herbert H. Hyman, "England and America: Climates of Tolerance and Intolerance," in Daniel Bell, ed., *The Radical Right* (Garden City, NY: Anchor Books, 1964), 305.

5 Edward Luce, *The Retreat of Western Liberalism* (New York: Atlantic Monthly Press, 2017).

6 Mary McCarthy to Hannah Arendt, April 26, 1951, in Carol Brightman, ed., *Between Friends: The Correspondence of Hannah Arendt and Mary McCarthy, 1949–1973* (New York: Harcourt Brace, 1995), 1.

7 Hannah Arendt, *The Origins of Totalitarianism* (Cleveland and New York: Meridian Books, 1951), 308.

8 Hannah Arendt, "We Refugees," in Marc Robinson, ed., *Altogether Elsewhere: Writers on Exile* (London and Boston: Faber and Faber, 1994), 116.

9 Arendt, *Origins*, 315.

10 José Ortega y Gasset, *The Revolt of the Masses* (1932; New York: Norton, 1957).

11 Arendt, *Origins*, 323, 339.

12 Arendt, *Origins*, 316.

13 Daniel Bell, "America as a Mass Society," in *The End of Ideology* (Glencoe: The Free Press, 1960), 21.

14 Seymour Martin Lipset, *Political Man: The Social Bases of Politics* (Garden City, NY: Anchor Books, 1960), 53.

15 William Kornhauser, *The Politics of Mass Society* (Glencoe: The Free Press, 1959), 76.

16 Macdonald, *Against the American Grain*, 55.

17 Macdonald, *Against the American Grain*, 24, 73.

18 Matthew Arnold, *Culture and Anarchy* (1869; New Haven: Yale University Press, 1994), 5.

19 Macdonald, *Against the American Grain*, 70–71.

20 Macdonald, *Against the American Grain*, 25.

21 Arlie Russell Hochschild, *Strangers in Their Own Land: Anger and Mourning on the American Right* (New York and London: New Press, 2016).
22 Bethany Moreton, *To Serve God and Wal-Mart: The Making of Christian Free Enterprise* (Cambridge, MA: Harvard University Press, 2009).
23 Katherine J. Cramer, *The Politics of Resentment: Rural Consciousness in Wisconsin and the Rise of Scott Walker* (Chicago: University of Chicago Press, 2016).
24 J. D. Vance, *Hillbilly Elegy: A Memoir of a Family and Culture in Crisis* (New York: HarperCollins, 2016).
25 Moreton, *To Serve God*, 104.
26 Hochschild, *Strangers*, 131.
27 Moreton, *To Serve God*, 15, 125.
28 Cramer, *Politics of Resentment*, 57.
29 Arendt, *Origins*, 306–7.
30 Hochschild, *Strangers*, 135, 149.
31 Cramer, *Politics of Resentment*, 40, 162.
32 Hochschild, *Strangers*, 225.
33 Richard Rorty, "Religion as a Conversation-Stopper," in *Philosophy and Social Hope* (New York: Penguin, 1999), 168–74.
34 Hochschild, *Strangers*, 95–96.
35 John Tierney, "Which States Are Givers and Which Are Takers," *The Atlantic*, May 15, 2014, https://www.theatlantic.com/business/archive/2014/05/which-states-are-givers-and-which-are-takers/361668/.
36 Dr. H. D. McCarty, "The Razorback Rabbi," YouTube, https://www.youtube.com/playlist?list=PLfa7E4vsHd89JEAxGIqF-wgusSNYmGPBm.
37 Moreton, *To Serve God*, 96, 98.
38 See H. D. McCarty's webpage, "Who We Are," Ventures for Christ, http://venturesforchrist.com/who-we-are/.
39 Arendt, *Origins*, 317.
40 Arendt, *Origins*, 306.
41 Arendt, *Origins*, 331.
42 Hochschild, *Strangers*, 122.
43 Arendt, *Origins*, 296.
44 Seymour Martin Lipset, "The Sources of the 'Radical Right,'" in Bell, *Radical Right*, 344.
45 Lipset, *Political Man*, 52, 101, 115–16.
46 Their research is summarized in Ariel Malka and Yphtach Lelkes, "In a New Poll, Half of Republicans Say They Would Support Postponing the 2020 Election If Trump Proposed It," *Washington Post*, August 10, 2017, https://www.washingtonpost.com/news/monkey-cage/wp/2017/08/10/in-a-new-poll-half-of-republicans-say-they-would-support-postponing-the-2020-election-if-trump-proposed-it/?utm_term=.0d1ee8681aeb.
47 S. M. Miller and Frank Riessman, "'Working-Class Authoritarianism': A Critique of Lipset," *British Journal of Sociology* 12 (September 1961): 271–72.
48 Peter Steinfels, *The Neoconservatives* (New York: Simon and Schuster, 1979), 4.
49 Thomas B. Edsall, "The Great Democratic Inversion," *New York Times*, Octo-

ber 27, 2016, https://www.nytimes.com/2016/10/27/opinion/campaign-stops/the-great-democratic-inversion.html.

50 Robert A. Dahl, *Who Governs: Democracy and Power in an American City* (New Haven: Yale University Press, 1961); E. E. Schattshneider, *The Semi-Sovereign People: A Realist's View of American Democracy* (New York: Holt, 1961); Joseph Schumpeter, *Capitalism, Socialism, and Democracy* (New York: Harper, 1950).

51 Steven Levitsky and Daniel Ziblatt, *How Democracies Die* (New York: Crown, 2018).

52 David Riesman, with Nathan Glazer and Reuel Denny, *The Lonely Crowd: A Study of the Changing American Character* (New Haven: Yale University Press, 1950), 152, 181, 201.

53 Richard Hofstadter, "Pseudo-Conservatism Revisited," in Bell, *Radical Right*, 102.

54 "Daily Chart: Democracy Continues Its Disturbing Retreat," *The Economist*, January 31, 2018, https://www.economist.com/blogs/graphicdetail/2018/01/daily-chart-21.

Chapter Four

1 These words helped shape the title of one of the best books on the whole subject of McCarthy and his life: David M. Oshinsky, *A Conspiracy So Immense: The World of Joe McCarthy* (New York: Free Press, 1983).

2 These examples can be found in Richard Hofstadter, *The Paranoid Style in American Politics, and Other Essays* (1955; New York: Vintage Books, 2008), 14, 29.

3 Phyllis Schlafly, *A Choice Not an Echo* (Alton, IL: Pere Marquette Press, 1964).

4 Richard Hofstadter, *The Paranoid Style in American Politics* (1965; Chicago: University of Chicago Press, 1979), 21.

5 Hofstadter, *Paranoid Style*, 24, 31.

6 Hofstadter, *Paranoid Style*, 3, 40.

7 Joseph E. Usinscky and Joseph M. Parent, *American Conspiracy Theories* (New York: Oxford University Press, 2014).

8 J. Eric Oliver and Thomas J. Wood, "Conspiracy Theories and the Paranoid Style(s) of Mass Opinion," *American Journal of Political Science* 58 (October 2014): 952–66.

9 Karlyn Bowman and Andrew Rugg, "Public Opinion on Conspiracy Theories," American Enterprise Institute, November 7, 2013, http://www.aei.org/publication/public-opinion-on-conspiracy-theories.

10 Sander van der Linden, "The Conspiracy Effect: Exposure to Conspiracy Theories (about Global Warming) Decreases Pro-Social Behavior and Science Acceptance," *Personality and Individual Differences* 87 (December 2015): 171–73.

11 Kate Starbird, "Examining the Alternative Media Ecosystem through the Production of Alternative Narratives of Mass Shooting Events on Twitter," https://faculty.washington.edu/kstarbi/Alt_Narratives_ICWSM17-CameraReady.pdf.

12 Cass Sunstein, *Conspiracy Theories and Other Dangerous Ideas* (New York: Simon and Schuster, 2014), 1–32.

13 For data on this, see Gordon Gauchet, "Politicization of Science in the Public Sphere: A Study of Public Trust in the United States, 1974–2010," *American Sociological Review* 77 (2012): 167–87.

14 Chris Mooney, *The Republican War on Science* (New York: Basic Books, 2005).

15 Matthew Motta, "The Dynamics and Political Implications of Anti-Intellectualism in the United States," *American Politics Research*, July 11, 2017, http://journals.sagepub.com/doi/full/10.1177/1532673X17719507.

16 Jon Stone, "Louise Mensch Claims She Has Evidence That the Founder of Breitbart Was Murdered by Russian Agents," *The Independent*, March 12, 2017, http://www.independent.co.uk/news/uk/politics/louise-mensch-andrew-breitbart-murder-conspiracy-theory-killed-a7625381.html.

17 Louise Mensch, "Britain Better Off Out of Europe," *New York Times*, February 13, 2016; Mensch, "What to Ask about Russian Hacking," *New York Times*, March 17, 2017.

18 See, for example, Bill Palmer, "Donald Trump Has Panicked Meltdown about Pee Pee Tape," The Palmer Report, http://www.palmerreport.com/politics/pee-trump-meltdown/6924/.

19 John F. Kennedy, *Profiles in Courage* (New York: Harper, 1956).

20 Hofstadter, *Paranoid Style*, 40.

21 John Kenneth Galbraith, *The Affluent Society* (1958; Boston: Houghton Mifflin, 1998), 6–17.

22 Irving Howe, "This Age of Conformity," *Partisan Review* 21 (January–February 1954), https://www.dissentmagazine.org/online_articles/irving-howe-voice-still-heard-this-age-of-conformity.

23 James A. Weschler, *The Age of Suspicion* (New York: Random House, 1963).

24 Bell, *End of Ideology*, 287.

25 Lionel Trilling, "Mansfield Park," in *The Opposing Self* (1955; New York: Harcourt Brace Jovanovich, 1978), 181, 185–86.

26 Reinhold Niebuhr, "The Irony of American History," in Elisabeth Sifton, ed., Reinhold Niebuhr, *Major Works on Religion and Politics* (New York: Library of America, 2015), 513, 585–86.

27 Richard Rorty, *Contingency, Irony, and Solidarity* (New York: Cambridge University Press, 1989), 73, 93.

28 Lionel Trilling, *A Gathering of Fugitives* (New York: Oxford University Press, 1980), 91, 103.

29 Niebuhr, *Major Works*, 508.

30 Benjamin DeMott, "Rediscovering Complexity," *The Atlantic*, September 1988, 67.

31 Daniel Patrick Moynihan, "The Professionalization of Reform," *The Public Interest* 1 (Fall 1965): 6–16.

32 Daniel Patrick Moynihan, "The Negro Family: The Case for National Action," https://web.stanford.edu/~mrosenfe/Moynihan%27s%20The%20Negro%20Family.pdf.

33 Daniel P. Moynihan to Richard M. Nixon, January 16, 1970, Nixon Library, https://www.nixonlibrary.gov/virtuallibrary/releases/ju110/53.pdf.

34 On Obama's understanding of irony, see R. Wald Holder and Peter B. Jacobsen, *The Irony of Barack Obama: Barack Obama, Reinhold Niebuhr, and the Problem of Christian Statecraft* (New York: Routledge, 2012).

Chapter Five

1 Reinhold Niebuhr, *Discerning the Signs of the Times: Sermons for Today and Tomorrow* (New York: Scribner's, 1946), 112.

2 Reinhold Niebuhr, "The Irony of American History," in Elisabeth Sifton, ed., Reinhold Niebuhr, *Major Works on Religion and Politics* (New York: Library of America, 2015), 465.

3 Dwight Macdonald, "Norman Cousin's Flat World," in *Masscult and Midcult: Essays against the American Grain*, ed. John Summers (New York: New York Review of Books, 2011), 269–89.

4 Lionel Trilling, *A Gathering of Fugitives* (New York: Oxford University Press, 1980), 71.

5 Trilling, *Gathering*, 70.

6 Lionel Trilling, *The Liberal Imagination: Essays on Literature and Society* (New York: Viking, 1950), 94.

7 Trilling, *Liberal Imagination*, 108.

8 Lionel Trilling, "A Triumph of the Comic View," in Arthur Krystal, ed., *A Company of Readers: Uncollected Writings of W. H. Auden, Jacques Barzun, and Lionel Trilling from the Readers' Subscription and Mid-Century Book Clubs* (New York: The Free Press, 2001), 106.

9 For Viereck's use of both terms, see George H. Nash, *The Conservative Intellectual Movement in America since 1945* (New York: Basic Books, 1976), 80, 150.

10 Peter Viereck, "The Revolt against the Elite," in Daniel Bell, ed., *The Radical Right* (Garden City, NY: Anchor Books, 1964), 179.

11 "American Sense of Alienation Remains at Record Highs," The Harris Poll, July 28, 2016, http://www.theharrispoll.com/politics/Americans-Alienation-Remains-Record-High.html.

12 Edmund Burke, "Reflections on the Revolution in France," in Isaac Kranmick, ed., *The Portable Edmund Burke* (New York: Penguin 1999), 467–68.

13 Joseph de Maistre, *The Executioner* (London: Penguin Book, 1993), 30, 68.

14 Louis Hartz, *The Liberal Tradition in America: An Interpretation of American Political Thought since the Revolution* (San Diego and New York: Harcourt, Brace, 1955), 181.

15 Nash, *Conservative Intellectual Movement.*

16 John Patrick Diggins, *Ronald Reagan: Fate, Freedom, and the Making of History* (New York: Norton, 2007).

17 Lionel Trilling, *Beyond Culture: Essays on Literature and Learning* (New York: Viking, 1965), xv-xvi.

18 Edmund Burke, "Speech at Mr. Burke's Arrival in Bristol," in Kranmick, *Portable Edmund Burke*, 156.

19 For a defense of Cleon, at least on the charge that he was in it for the money, see T. A. Dorey, "Aristophanes and Cleon," *Greece and Rome* 3 (1956): 132–39.

20 Aristophanes, *The Knights*, http://classics.mit.edu/Aristophanes/knights.html.

21 Terry Lindvall, *God Mocks: A History of Religious Satire from the Hebrew Prophets to Stephen Colbert* (New York: New York University Press, 2015), 87, 88.

22 Peter Berger, *Redeeming Laughter: The Comic Dimension of Human Experience* (New York: Walter de Gruyter, 1997).

23 Maurice Joly, *Dialogue aux Enfer Entre Machiavel et Montesquieu, ou La Politique de Machiavel au XIXe Sièicle, par un Contemporain* (Brussels: Mertens et fils, 1864), 53, 99.

24 Alexis de Tocqueville, *Democracy in America*, Phillips Bradley Edition (New York; Knopf, 1966), 2:139.

25 For a recent biography, see Fiona Deans Halloran, *Thomas Nast: The Father of Political Cartoons* (Chapel Hill: University of North Carolina Press, 2012).

26 Kliph Nesteroff, *The Comedians: Drunks, Thieves, Scoundrels, and the History of American Comedy* (New York: Grove Press, 2015), 20.

27 Mary Gluck, *The Invisible Jewish Budapest: Metropolitan Culture at the Fin de Siècle* (Madison: University of Wisconsin Press, 2016).

28 This remark has been cited by many. See, for example, Wes D. Gehring, *Film Clowns of the Depression: Twelve Defining Comic Performances* (Jefferson, NC: McFarland, 2007), 2.

29 Luke Epplin, "What the Marx Brothers' *Duck Soup* Can Teach Us about Trump," *Brow Beat* (blog), Slate, August 31, 2016, http://www.slate.com/blogs/browbeat/2016/08/31/what_the_marx_brothers_duck_soup_can_teach_us_about_trump.html.

30 See Jody C. Baumgartner and Jonathan S. Morris, eds., *Laughing Matters: Humor and Politics in the Media Age* (New York: Routledge, 2008); Amarnath Amarasingham, ed., *The Stewart/Colbert Effect: Essays on the Real Impacts of Fake News* (Jefferson, NC: McFarland, 2011); and Sophia A. McLennan and Remy Maisel, *Is Satire Saving Our Nation? Mockery and America Politics* (New York: Palgrave Macmillan, 2014).

31 Jonathan Chait, "Not a Very P.C. Thing to Say: How the Language Police Are Perverting Liberalism," *New York*, January 27, 2015, http://nymag.com/daily/intelligencer/2015/01/not-a-very-pc-thing-to-say.html.

32 Mark Lilla, *The Once and Future Liberal: After Identity Politics* (New York: Harpers, 2017), 10.

33 Daniel Patrick Moynihan, "Defining Deviance Down," *American Scholar* 62 (Winter 1993): 17–30.

34 Todd van Luling, "Senator Al Franken Doesn't Think Donald Trump Is 'Funny at All,' Except This One Time," *Huffington Post*, August 2, 2017, http://www.huffingtonpost.com/entry/al-franken-funny-donald-trump_us_5981dd79e4b02b36343f457.

35 Reinhold Niebuhr, *Beyond Tragedy: Essays on the Christian Interpretation of History* (New York: Scribner's 1937), 151.

36 Arthur Schlesinger Jr., *The Cycles of American History* (Boston: Houghton Mifflin, 1986).

Chapter Six

1 See the suggestive title of political scientist Michael Tesler's book *Post-Racial or Most-Racial: Race and Politics in the Obama Years* (Chicago: University of Chicago Press, 2016).

2 Michael Tesler, "Views about Race Mattered More in Electing Trump Than in Electing Obama," *Washington Post*, November 22, 2016, https://www.washingtonpost.com/news/monkey-cage/wp/2016/11/22/peoples-views-about-race-mattered-more-in-electing-trump-than-in-electing-obama/?utm_term=.6904b59f6de7.

3 Thomas Wood, "Racism Motivated Trump Voters More Than Authoritarianism," *Washington Post*, April 17, 2017, https://www.washingtonpost.com/news/monkey-cage/wp/2017/04/17/racism-motivated-trump-voters-more-than-authoritarianism-or-income-inequality/?utm_term=.a2e783e7fe08.

4 Bernard L. Fraga, Sean McElwee, Jesse Rhodes, and Brian Shaffner, "Why Did Trump Win? More Whites—and Fewer Blacks—Actually Voted," *Washington Post*, May 8, 2017, https://www.washingtonpost.com/news/monkey-cage/wp/2017/04/17/racism-motivated-trump-voters-more-than-authoritarianism-or-income-inequality/?utm_term=.a2e783e7fe08.

5 Katherine J. Cramer, *The Politics of Resentment: Rural Consciousness in Wisconsin and the Rise of Scott Walker* (Chicago: University of Chicago Press, 2016), 84.

6 Arlie Russell Hochschild, *Strangers in Their Own Land: Anger and Mourning on the American Right* (New York and London: New Press, 2016), 114.

7 See the discussion of this issue by Jeff Stein, "The Bernie Voters Who Defected to Trump Explained by a Political Scientist, Vox, August 24, 2017, https://www.vox.com/policy-and-politics/2017/8/24/16194086/bernie-trump-voters-study.

8 The term originated as "low-information rationality" in the work of Samuel Popkin, *The Reasoning Voter: Communication and Persuasion in Presidential Campaigns* (Chicago: University of Chicago Press, 1991).

9 Meredith Dost, "Dim Public Awareness of Supreme Court as Major Rulings Loom," Pew Research Center, May 14, 2015, http://www.pewresearch.org/fact-tank/2015/05/14/dim-public-awareness-of-supreme-court-as-major-rulings-loom/.

10 Ilya Somin, *Democracy and Political Ignorance: Why Smaller Government Is Smarter*, 2nd ed. (Stanford: Stanford University Press, 2016), 1.

11 Richard C. Fording and Sanford F. Schram, "The Cognitive and Emotional Sources of Trump Support: The Case of Low Information Voters," *New Political Science* 5 (October 2017): 1–17.

12 Rebecca Savransky, "Cruz: Trump Supporters are 'Low Information Voters,'" The Hill, March 10, 2016, http://thehill.com/blogs/ballot-box/presidential-races/272497-cruz-trump-supporters-are-low-information-voters.

13 Josh Hafner, "Donald Trump Loves the 'Poorly Educated'—and They Love Him," *USA Today*, February 24, 2016, https://www.usatoday.com/story/news/politics/onpolitics/2016/02/24/donald-trump-nevada-poorly-educated/80860078/.

14 "Election 2016: Exit Polls," *New York Times*, November 8, 2016, https://www.nytimes.com/interactive/2016/11/08/us/politics/election-exit-polls.html?_r=0.

15 My favorite account is Susan Jacoby, *The Age of American Unreason* (New York: Vintage, 2008).

16 Charles Taylor, with Anthony Appiah, Jürgen Habermas, and Steven Rockefeller, *Multiculturalism: Examining the Politics of Recognition* (Princeton: Princeton University Press, 1994).

17 Florida Department of State, Division of Elections, *Proposed Constitutional Amendments to Be Voted On, November 8, 2016*, http://dos.myflorida.com/media/696216/constitutional-amendments-2016-general-english-booklet.pdf.

18 Arthur Lupia, "Shortcuts versus Encyclopedia: Information and Voting Behavior in California Insurance Reform Elections," *American Political Science Review* 88 (March 1994): 63–76.

19 See Somin, *Democracy*; and Jason Brennan, *Against Democracy* (Princeton: Princeton University Press. 2016).

20 Cara C. Tigue, Diana J. Borak, Jillian J. M. O'Connor, Charles Schandl, and David R. Feinberg, "Voice Pitch Influences Voting Behavior," *Evolution and Human Behavior* 3 (May 2012): 210–16.

21 Howard Gardner, *Frames of Mind: The Theory of Multiple Intelligences* (New York: Basic Books, 1983).

22 James Bryce, *The American Commonwealth*, vol. 1, *The National Government—The State Governments*, 3rd ed. (New York and London: Macmillan, 1895), 80.

23 James Kirchik, *The End of Europe: Dictators, Demagogues, and the Coming Dark Age* (New Haven: Yale University Press, 2017); and Ivan Krastev, *After Europe* (Philadelphia: University of Pennsylvania Press, 2017). For a more positive assessment of immigration to Europe, see Sasha Polakow-Suransky, *Go Back to Where You Came From: The Backlash against Immigration and the Fate of Western Democracy* (New York: Nation Books, 2107).

24 Roberto Stefan Foa and Yascha Mounk, "The Democratic Discontent," *Journal of Democracy* 27 (July 2016): 7. Roberto Stefan Foa and Yascha Mounk, "The Danger of Deconsolidation: The Democratic Discontent," *Journal of Democracy* 27 (July 2016): 7. See also Yascha Mounk, *The People versus Democracy: Why Our Freedom Is in Danger and How to Save It* (Cambridge, MA: Harvard University Press, 2018).

25 Amy C. Alexander and Christian Welzel, "The Myth of Deconsolidation: Rising Liberalism and the Populist Reaction," *Journal of Democracy*, https://www.journalofdemocracy.org/sites/default/files/media/Journal%20of%20Democracy%20Web%20Exchange%20-%20Alexander%20and%20Welzel.pdf; Pippa Norris, "Is Western Democracy Backsliding: Diagnosing the Risks," *Journal of Democracy*, https://www.journalofdemocracy.org/sites/default/files/media/Journal%20of%20Democracy%20Web%20Exchange%20-%20Norris_0.pdf; and Eric Voeten, "Are People Turning Away from Democracy?," *Journal of Democracy*, https://www.journalofdemocracy.org/sites/default/files/media/Journal%20of%20Democracy%20Web%20Exchange%20-%20Voeten_0.pdf.

26 Paul Howe, "Eroding Norms and Democratic Deconsolidation," *Journal of Democracy* 28 (October 2017): 23.

27 Fareed Zakaria, "Populism on the March: Why the West Is in Trouble," *Foreign Affairs* 95 (November–December 2016): 9.

Chapter Seven

1 Timothy Snyder, *On Tyranny: Twenty Lessons from the Twentieth Century* (New York: Tim Duggan Books, 2017).

2 "Limbaugh Unloads: Obama a 'Petulant, Self-Absorbed, Egoistic Little Man-Child,'" Fox Nation, July 26, 2011, http://nation.foxnews.com/rush-limbaugh/2011/07/26/limbaugh-unloads-obama-petulant-self-absorbed-egoistic-little-man-child.

3 Daniel Bell, "The End of Ideology," in *The End of Ideology* (Glencoe: The Free Press, 1960), 375.

4 Michael Oakeshott (?), "Political Maturity," Michael Oakeshott Association, http://www.michael-oakeshott-association.com/pdfs/mo_political_maturity.pdf.

5 Charles J. Sykes, *How the Right Lost Its Mind* (New York: St. Martin's, 2017), 107, 222.

6 Richard Hofstadter, *The Age of Reform: From Bryan to F.D.R.* (New York: Vintage Books, 1995), 174–214.

7 "What Is Civility," Institute for Civility in Government, http://www.instituteforcivility.org/who-we-are/what-is-civility/.

8 For some evidence for this conclusion, see Joseph E. Usinscky and Joseph M. Parent, *American Conspiracy Theories* (New York: Oxford University Press, 2014).

9 Kevin Williamson, "Preparing for the Presidential Debates," *National Review*, September 25, 2016, http://www.nationalreview.com/article/440373/presidential-debates-spectacle-they-are-not-debates.

10 Bill Moyers and Michael Winship, "There's No Debate," Moyers & Company, http://billmoyers.com/story/theres-no-debate/.

11 Julia R. Azari and Jennifer K. Smith, "Unwritten Rules in Established Democracies," *Perspectives on Politics* 10 (March 2012): 37–55, https://www.cambridge.org/core/journals/perspectives-on-politics/article/unwritten-rules-informal-institutions-in-established-democracies/E4B2DE0BA67180E3C63ED7852FB0EA56.

12 Stephen F. Cohen, "US Double Standards in the New Cold War," *The Nation*, October 25, 2017, https://www.thenation.com/article/us-double-standards-in-the-new-cold-war/.

13 E. J. Dionne Jr., Norman J. Ornstein, and Thomas E. Mann, *One Nation after Trump: A Guide for the Perplexed, the Disillusioned, the Desperate, and the Not-Yet Deported* (New York: St. Martin's Press, 2017).

14 Kurt Andersen, *Fantasyland: How America Went Haywire* (New York: Random House, 2017).

INDEX